This is one of several booklets *The Voice of Elijah* distributes free of charge to anyone who requests a copy. The mission of *The Voice of Elijah* is to educate the public in regard to Early Church teaching that the Church has long since lost. The following six titles are currently available. You may request them either by writing directly to the publisher or by typing your name and address into the form found on *The Voice of Elijah* web site—*www.voiceofelijah.org*:

The AntiChrist
The Passover Parable
Wanna Hear a Whopper?
7 Simple Steps to Salvation
In the Image and Likeness of God
The Old Testament Gospel of Jesus Christ

Wanna

Hear

a

Whopper?

Larry D. Harper

The
Elijah
Project

Mesquite, Texas

CONTENTS

INTRODUCTION 1
LET'S DEFINE A FEW TERMS 7
THE TRIBULATION AND THE RAPTURE 8
SO CLOSE, YET SO FAR APART 11
THE ORIGINS OF COVENANT THEOLOGY 12
COVENANT THEOLOGY IN BRIEF 13
THE EARLY CHURCH FATHERS 15
A HINT OF THINGS TO COME 18
THE ORIGIN OF DISPENSATIONAL THEOLOGY 19
DISPENSATIONAL THEOLOGY IN BRIEF 25
TWO VIEWS, ONE POINT OF DISAGREEMENT 28
THE RAPTURE OF THE SAINTS 29
THE SPREAD OF DISPENSATIONALISM 31
THE NIAGARA BIBLE CONFERENCE 33
ARNO C. GAEBELEIN 35
THE SCOFIELD REFERENCE BIBLE 37
EVANGELISTS AND DISPENSATIONALISM 40
THE BIBLE INSTITUTE MOVEMENT 41
SECOND THOUGHTS 44
A GLIMPSE INTO SATAN'S PLAN 46
SATAN'S PLANNED DECEPTION 49
A FINAL WARNING 50
FINAL COMMENTS 51

WANNA HEAR A WHOPPER?[1]

Introduction

Have you ever noticed that when folks *talk about* Satan they tend to talk in terms of haunted houses, demon possession, and the rituals of satanic cults? That's the way Satan wants it. While those things may well tell us a bit about what he does, they certainly don't tell us who he is. But Satan doesn't want us to know who he is or, for that matter, all that much about what he does. He knows that if we knew the Truth, it could (and would) thwart what he has planned. So we have to look a bit deeper than demon possession and satanic rituals to uncover what Satan has been up to recently.

Satan can be aptly described in many different ways. A few of the more select terms that readily come to mind are moron, idiot, imbecile, lamebrain, and dolt. But that is only because he has chosen not to believe the Truth. None of these terms accurately capture the essence of his nature. For that, one must resort to the four-letter word *liar*. Should you doubt that, let me remind you of what Jesus rather rudely told some of His contemporaries:

> *"You are of {your} father the devil, and you want to do the desires of your father. He was a murderer from the beginning, and does not stand in the truth, because there is no truth in him. **Whenever he speaks a lie, he***

---

[1] This book contains a reprint of an article titled "Wanna Hear the Whopper the Liar Came Up With? (I Doubt You'll Believe It!)" *The Voice of Elijah*, October 1996.

speaks from his own {nature}; for he is a liar, and the father of lies."
(John 8:44)

What Jesus said in that verse applies to anyone who rejects the Truth when they have the opportunity to hear it. But that's not the point I want to make. When you hear that verse mentioned, you probably also hear the well-worn story about how Satan deceived Eve and that's the end of it. When was the last time anyone told you Satan is still alive and well, deceiving people all the time? When have you been warned to carefully examine what you believe lest you, too, be deceived by the Liar? But more to the point, when have you ever considered the possibility that Satan might already have you believing one of his lies?

If you have never been warned that you might be caught in Satan's web, you are certainly being warned now. Satan is well on his way toward accomplishing his greatest deception exactly as the Scriptures tell us he will before the End. So you had best take heed if you know what's good for you. But before I get into explaining Satan's deception, let me remind you what the Scriptures have to say about the Liar's plan.

In the Book of Revelation, the Apostle John refers to Satan's deception in three different places. The first is in his description of how Satan comes to be on Earth:

*And the great dragon was thrown down, the serpent of old who is called the devil and **Satan, who deceives the whole world**; he was thrown down to the earth, and his angels were thrown down with him.*
(Revelation 12:9)

John's second reference to Satan's great, grand, and—as he believes—glorious deception can be found in a passage where John describes events that will occur when the Antichrist appears:

***And he deceives those who dwell on the earth** because of the signs which it was given him to perform in the presence of the beast, telling those who dwell on the earth to make an image to the beast who had the wound of the sword and has come to life.*
(Revelation 13:14)

John's final mention of Satan's deception occurs in his account of Satan's imprisonment:

And I saw an angel coming down from heaven, having the key of the abyss and a great chain in his hand. And he laid hold of the dragon, the serpent of

*old, who is the devil and Satan, and bound him for a thousand years, and threw him into the abyss, and shut {it} and sealed {it} over him, **so that he should not deceive the nations any longer,** until the thousand years were completed; after these things he must be released for a short time.*
(Revelation 20:1–3)

These are not the only places in the Scriptures where Satan's deception is mentioned, however. The Prophets *talk about* it all the time. For the most part, they refer to his deceit only cryptically, and they describe it in terms of *parabolic imagery.* The Apostle Paul does that as well, but he also outlines it openly in what he says concerning the Antichrist:

*And then that lawless one will be revealed whom the Lord will slay with the breath of His mouth and bring to an end by the appearance of His coming; {that is,} the one whose coming is in accord with the activity of Satan, with all power and signs and false wonders, **and with all the deception of wickedness for those who perish, because they did not receive the love of the truth so as to be saved. And for this reason God will send upon them a deluding influence so that they might believe what is false, in order that they all may be judged who did not believe the truth, but took pleasure in wickedness.***
(2 Thessalonians 2:8–12)

So there you have it. The Scriptures plainly tell us Satan, in keeping with his character as the consummate Liar, is planning to do his best to wrap things up all neat and tidy here at the End by foisting off one whale of a deception on those who don't want to know the Truth. Now, we know from what Jesus said that Satan is first and foremost a liar, and we also know from what the Apostles John and Paul tell us that he plans to "deceive the whole world" when he appears in the person of the Antichrist. So it makes sense to me (but perhaps not to you) that Satan would try to accomplish that by corrupting the Truth God has revealed in the Scriptures. That is, we should logically expect him, in whatever way he possibly can, to be constantly working to distort what Jesus Christ instructed the Church to teach.[2] You may choose to believe otherwise. If so, I have no doubt you are of the same mind as those to whom Jesus was speaking when He called Satan a liar.

The Truth is, Satan has already put in place the deception by which he intends to "deceive the whole world." It exists in the form of a teaching that has, like the tentacles of an octopus, spread throughout

---

[2] Matthew 28:18–20.

the Evangelical wing of the Protestant Church. It has been ensnaring True Believers one by one for the past 170 years. Therefore, most Christians today have unwittingly accepted Satan's lie without even knowing what it is or how it got into the Church. That's why I'm going to tell you what you need to know about Satan's lie. Then, if you don't believe me, I won't be responsible for you being taken in by it.

If you doubt that Satan could ever accomplish what I just described, you really should wake up and smell the barnyard. Why do you think the Eastern Orthodox and Roman Catholic Churches teach so many different doctrines? What reason do you give for the fact that the Protestant Church believes things the Roman Catholic Church hasn't given much more than lip service to since the fourth century? I won't even bother to remind you there are thousands of Protestant denominations and sects that hold some ridiculous belief that nobody had ever heard of until their founder thought it up. I'll simply tell you that if you deny that Satan has been fostering false doctrine in the Church and still claim to be a Protestant, you need to have someone replace your central processing unit or, at the very least, upgrade your memory. Your equipment is quite obviously malfunctioning.

The Protestant Reformers—you know, the men who gave rise to the Protestant Church—all believed the leaders of the Roman Catholic Church were teaching false doctrines because Satan had deceived them. That is the reason they gave for their assertion that the Church had lost the Truth they claimed to be restoring. As a matter of fact, until the beginning of the twentieth century, many in the Protestant Church continued to believe the Church had lost some essential belief that still needed to be restored. [3]

By 1900, however, when Pentecostals decided their doctrine concerning the "baptism of the Holy Spirit" was the one remaining thing the Church had lost, the Protestant Church, for the most part, had given up trying to *restore* lost Truth. Consequently, today we face the sad situation in which idiots who claim to be Protestant reject their own heritage by denouncing anyone who claims the Church ever lost anything. Those who hold that view merely reveal their ignorance of Church history.

Any born-again Believer with even a shred of common sense should be able to see that Satan has deceived the Church to one degree or another over the past eighteen hundred years, ever since the Early

---

[3] See "The Protestant Confession: The Church Lost *The Teaching*" and "One Train. One Track. Two Rails." *The Voice of Elijah*, January 1992 and "Protestants All Agree on This: Somebody Laid an Egg!" *The Voice of Elijah*, January 1994.

Church "turned aside from *The Way*" under the tutelage of Origen the Idiot.[4] That has in no way thwarted God's plan and purpose for the Church, however, because the Church has, in every generation, still had "the Many" who have understood and believed the Truth of the Gospel. That will not change even at the height of Satan's deception here at the End. After all, God has ways of accomplishing things that Satan would like to think are impossible.

You must understand I use the term *gospel* to mean the basic Truth concerning Jesus Christ that one must believe in order to be born again.[5] However, I make that distinction here only because I am going to use it to show you how Satan has crafted a delusion that has already deceived most born-again Believers in our own generation. He has done so by making sure his delusion is preached right alongside the Gospel. Even that unhappy circumstance would not be so troublesome were it not for the fact that Satan intends to use his lie to completely invalidate one central Truth that all True Believers believe about Jesus Christ. As Jesus warned us, Satan will do that by pretending to be Jesus Christ Himself:

> *"Then if anyone says to you, 'Behold, here is the Christ,' or 'There {He is},' do not believe {him}. For false Christs and false prophets will arise and will show great signs and wonders, so as to mislead, if possible, even the elect. Behold, I have told you in advance."*
> *(Matthew 24:23–25)*

Please don't misunderstand me. God has in all ages redeemed a multitude who believed far greater lies and understood much less Truth than True Believers do today. So whether or not one believes a lie is not the issue. The essence of the problem has to do with the content of the lie that one chooses to believe. Look at it logically: If we had to believe the whole Truth and nothing but the Truth in order to be saved, none of us could be saved. Paul plainly tells us we know only "in part."[6] Yet there is obviously a bare minimum of Truth that one must believe in order to be saved. Otherwise, we could be saved—as some morons in the Church today would have us understand—by believing nothing at all.

---

[4] See "Did You *Mean* That Literally?" and "The Origen of Folly," *The Voice of Elijah*, January 1993.

[5] See "What's Left of the Right That Stayed Down When He Went Up?" *The Voice of Elijah Update*, September 1995, which has also been reprinted in the booklet titled *7 Simple Steps to Salvation.*

[6] 1 Corinthians 13:9, 12.

The Truth is, Satan's lies are a problem for True Believers only when they cause them to give up some essential Truth. That is why the Protestant Church has repeatedly identified eschatology[7] as an area in which one's beliefs are not essential to salvation. I will readily admit that has been the case until now, but what has been is about to change. And I warn you, if you don't pay attention when attention is due, you will pay the debt you owe God with something you deem much more valuable later on. Having said that, I have exonerated myself and made you responsible for whether or not you choose to believe the things I am going to tell you now.

You see, we all act in accordance with what we believe. Since I have explained that concept repeatedly in other places, I need not dwell on it here.[8] Satan knows our beliefs determine our actions. So it's too bad for you if you don't, because he fully intends to make you act in accordance with his lie.

I only mention the relationship between beliefs and actions because, for the past 170 years, Satan has been herding the Church toward a circumstance wherein the beliefs you hold concerning the Second Coming of Christ are going to determine your eternal destiny. If that sounds ridiculous to you, read on. Perhaps you will get a chuckle out of the things God has called me to proclaim. But before you enjoy a good, hearty laugh at my expense, let me remind you of that eternal verity you may have forgotten: "It ain't over 'til the fat lady sings." That's just another way of saying the one who laughs last will laugh the loudest—and by far the longest—in the sweet by-and-by.

That proverbial fat lady hasn't even entered the theater. Yet. So by all means keep on laughing while time is still on your side. I am more than willing to let eternity tell which of us is the brainless one. As the saying goes, "It's not *what you don't know* that's dangerous, it's *what you think you know*." But that's just another way of putting an old adage I'm rather fond of: "Assumptions will kill you." So if you want to assume I'm just another religious crackpot, go right ahead. I'll be the first to admit it's your God-given right.

---

[7] Eschatology is the study of beliefs concerning the future of the Church.

[8] See the following articles in *The Voice of Elijah* newsletter: "The Demons Also Believe (Poor Devils!)" October 1991; "Nobody in Their Right Mind Would Even Want to Be Napoleon!" October 1992; "Watching Ducks Sashaying 'Round the CornerStone," April 1993; "Counterfeiters, Con Artists (and the Consummate Consumer)," July 1993; and "Satan's Fools Are Satan's Tools," April 1994.

Let's Define a Few Terms

Before we get into the details of Satan's lie, there are a few basic terms you need to understand. The first four terms I am going to define are associated with the thousand-year reign of Christ that John mentions in the Book of Revelation:

> And I saw an angel coming down from heaven, having the key of the abyss and a great chain in his hand. And he laid hold of the dragon, the serpent of old, who is the devil and Satan, and bound him for a thousand years, and threw him into the abyss, and shut {it} and sealed {it} over him, **so that he should not deceive the nations any longer, until the thousand years were completed;** after these things he must be released for a short time. And I saw thrones, and they sat upon them, and judgment was given to them. And I {saw} the souls of those who had been beheaded because of the testimony of Jesus and because of the word of God, and those who had not worshiped the beast or his image, and had not received the mark upon their forehead and upon their hand; **and they came to life and reigned with Christ for a thousand years.** The rest of the dead did not come to life until the thousand years were completed. This is the first resurrection. Blessed and holy is the one who has a part in the first resurrection; over these the second death has no power, but **they will be priests of God and of Christ and will reign with Him for a thousand years.**
> (Revelation 20:1–6)

The thousand-year period John mentions in this passage is commonly called the "Millennium." That term comes from a combination of the Latin words for "thousand" (*mille*) and "year" (*annus*). However, that's about the only thing related to the Millennium that church folks agree on. That's because, while John clearly speaks of a thousand-year reign of Christ, he does not specifically tell us *where* Christ reigns. Does He reign on Earth, in Heaven, or in the hearts of men?

The dispute over the place where Christ reigns may seem silly to some. It has nonetheless given rise to three different views concerning the time of His Return to the Earth. Those who think this passage tells us Christ will reign on Earth for a thousand years obviously believe He will return to Earth before the Millennium begins. This is the "premillennial" view. Not surprisingly, those who hold this view are called "premillennialists." I am one of those, but only because I agree with the Early Church Fathers Irenæus and Hippolytus.

There are those, however, who do not believe Christ will reign on Earth during the thousand-year period that John mentions. They believe

He won't return to Earth until the end of the Millennium. These folks hold what is called the "postmillennial" view and are, consequently, known as "postmillennialists." The postmillennial view originated with Daniel Whitby (1638–1726), rector of Salisbury, and became popular in the Protestant Church after it became obvious that the view of the Protestant Reformers was an innovation traceable to Augustine's time.

The third view, the one that Daniel Whitby found objectionable, is the "amillennial" view.[9] The people who hold this view are "amillennialists" because they don't even believe there is going to be a Millennium. That is, they don't think there is going to be a *literal* thousand-year reign of Christ on Earth, in Heaven, or anywhere else for that matter. Now, before you roundly denounce the amillennialists' view as ridiculous, perhaps you should consider the fact that they believe the thousand-year reign of Christ that John mentions in Revelation 20 conveys only the *symbolic meaning* that Christ will reign over a long span of time.

The traditional amillennial view is that Jesus Christ is already reigning on Earth in the Church. This belief originated with the African Donatist Tyconius around A.D. 380 and eventually replaced the original premillenial view of the Apostolic Church. Tyconius came to his understanding of Revelation 20 on the basis of Origen's goofy allegorical method of interpretation. Since Augustine (A.D. 354–430) was fond of Origen's allegorical method, he adopted Tyconius' amillennialism and popularized it, thereby making it the doctrine of the Roman Catholic Church.

So there you have it. Depending on who you choose to believe, there is either going to be a *literal* thousand-year reign of Christ—a Millennium—as the premillennialists and postmillennialists say there is. Or there is not going to be a clearly identifiable thousand-year reign as the amillennialists claim. The issue of whether or not there is a Millennium is more or less irrelevant to our discussion here. I mention it only because, before you can grasp the implications of what I have to say, you need to understand the following four terms: *Millennium, premillennial, postmillennial,* and *amillennial.*

The Tribulation and the Rapture

If you look closely at what John says concerning events leading up to the Millennium in Revelation 19 and 20, you will find that he tells

---

[9] The *a* in the word *amillennial* derives from a Greek prefix with the *meaning* "no."

us the deception of the Antichrist will end with the imprisonment of Satan at the Return of Jesus Christ:

> *And I saw an angel coming down from heaven, having the key of the abyss and a great chain in his hand. And he laid hold of the dragon, the serpent of old, who is the devil and Satan, and bound him for a thousand years, and threw him into the abyss, and shut {it} and sealed {it} over him, **so that he should not deceive the nations any longer, until the thousand years were completed;** after these things he must be released for a short time. (Revelation 20:1–3)*

That brings up yet another set of terms whose *meaning* and *significance* you must understand before I can explain how Satan intends to pull off the deception he has planned. So let me define those terms before I get into his goofiness.

First of all, the reign of the Antichrist is normally called "the Tribulation." Some folks call it "the Great Tribulation." Since the text above plainly says the deception of Satan will end with the Second Coming of Jesus Christ, most premillennialists (including the Early Church Fathers Irenæus and Hippolytus) correctly believe the Tribulation caused by the Antichrist will end right before the Millennium begins. But that's not what concerns the premillennialists. They believe the things described in the following passage go right to the heart of the matter:

> *But we do not want you to be uninformed, brethren, about those who are asleep, that you may not grieve, as do the rest who have no hope. For if we believe that Jesus died and rose again, even so God will bring with Him those who have fallen asleep in Jesus. For this we say to you by the word of the Lord, that we who are alive, and remain until the coming of the Lord, shall not precede those who have fallen asleep. For the Lord Himself will descend from heaven with a shout, with the voice of the archangel, and with the trumpet of God; and the dead in Christ shall rise first. **Then we who are alive and remain shall be caught up together with them in the clouds to meet the Lord in the air, and thus we shall always be with the Lord.** (1 Thessalonians 4:13–17)*

The event Paul mentions in verse 17 is called "the Rapture." The English word *rapture* comes from the Latin **rapio** which *means* to "seize or snatch." However, the New Testament was not written in Latin, it was written in Greek. And the Greek word translated "caught up" in verse 17 is **harpadzo**. It is the same word Luke used to describe the Spirit's relocation of Philip in Acts 8:39.

And when they came up out of the water, **the Spirit of the Lord snatched
Philip away; and the eunuch saw him no more,** *but went on his way
rejoicing.*
(Acts 8:39)

Obviously, if Luke could use the Greek word *harpadzo* to describe
the Spirit's transportation of Philip from one location to another on the
face of the Earth, Paul could just as easily use it to describe the event
known as "the Rapture." In Paul's case, however, *harpadzo* refers to the
transportation of True Believers from their various locations on the
ground to some central location "in the air." But even that is not the
central point of disagreement among premillennialists concerning
what Paul has said. You see, just as folks disagree about whether Christ
will return before or after the Millennium, premillennialists disagree as
to where the Rapture of the saints stands in relation to the Tribulation.
That's because, like John, Paul does not tell us precisely how the event
he describes fits together with the reign of the Antichrist.

Some premillennial folks believe the Rapture is going to occur
before the Tribulation caused by the Antichrist. These are called "pretribulationists." (If you want to sound really well-versed in the subject,
however, you can say they hold the "pretrib" position.) Not surprisingly, other premillennialists disagree with the pretribulationist view of
the Rapture. They say Christ will Rapture the saints at the end of the
Tribulation. So we call them "posttribulationists." Still others believe the
Rapture will occur sometime during the Tribulation. They are the
"midtribulationists."

So you see, there is a wide variety of perspectives in the Evangelical wing of the Protestant Church regarding the things the Scriptures
teach concerning the End, when Jesus Christ will Return and "snatch
away" His own just as Paul said He would. First of all, we have various
opinions concerning where the Return of Jesus Christ stands in relation to the Millennium. On that issue, some folks are premillennialists,
some postmillennialists, and some amillennialists. Then, in connection
with how premillennialists believe the Rapture stands in relation to the
Tribulation, some are pretribulationists, some posttribulationists, and
some midtribulationists.

Now, it would seem that all these fine folks disagree on a broad
spectrum of issues, but the Truth is, there are basically only two camps
into which all these varied viewpoints fall. And in spite of the fact that
each and every one of the members of these two camps argue their
case on a text-by-text basis, they all came to a general understanding of

those texts long before they ever got around to studying them in detail. That is, their beliefs as to the overall message of the Scriptures dictates how they believe individual passages speak concerning events that will occur at the End. I know that, however, only because I have spent a good bit of time reading the charges and countercharges the opposing camps have brought against each other.

I will tell you at the outset that, while the adherents of the two camps rightly criticize the opposing view, neither of the two groups has yet been able to discern the overall message of the Scriptures. That is why both sides have valid points to make in regard to the weaknesses they find in the other view. But the fact that these two camps can accurately point out the flaws they see in the other position does not mean their own position offers any better solution. It merely illustrates the fact that neither of the two sides has yet been able to discern the Truth. That's why I am going to explain the delusion Satan has worked to put in place over the past 170 years. Perhaps then you will be better able to see why you should not believe the things he would have you believe.

So Close, Yet So Far Apart

As I just said, there are only two basic views concerning the overall message of the Scriptures. The one understanding of what the Scriptures have to say is called Covenant, or Reformed, Theology. The other has become widely known as Dispensational Theology. While the members of these two camps disagree on all kinds of things related to the message of the Scriptures, they have already agreed they are in irreconcilable disagreement on only two essential points. Actually, one side says they disagree on two points. The other side says they disagree on only one. The Truth is, as usual, somewhere in between.

Covenant theologians say they are in implacable disagreement with dispensational theologians on the following two fundamental issues: (1) the *"literal"* method the dispensationalists say one must use to interpret the Scriptures and (2) the distinction the dispensationalists make between Israel and the Church. Yet covenant theologians have repeatedly pointed out that, in spite of the fact that dispensational theologians claim to use a *literal* method of interpreting Scripture, they actually use the same method of interpretation that covenant theologians use. So you will find dispensational theologians today hedging a bit on the issue of how *literal* their method of interpretation actually needs to be.

Because of their disagreement on these two basic issues, covenant and dispensational theologians hold widely divergent views concerning the future of the Church. So let's take a look at what the two sides have to say about the two points on which they claim to be in fundamental disagreement. Along the way, we will also look at the events they believe will precede the Second Coming of Jesus Christ. We can begin by surveying the origins of Covenant Theology.

The Origins of Covenant Theology

Covenant Theology originated with John Calvin, one of the leaders of the Protestant Reformation, as a complete systematic theology. But as I have mentioned repeatedly, John Calvin and the other Reformers believed they were restoring essential Truths that the Roman Catholic Church had lost.[10] So, in his battle against the obvious distortions of Truth he found in the Roman Catholic Church, Calvin sought authority for his views by appealing to the writings of the fourth century theologian Augustine. For that reason, Calvin's Covenant Theology is often called Augustinian Theology; and we must admit that, to the extent that it agrees with what Augustine wrote, Covenant Theology actually originated in the fourth century. However, Augustine agrees with the Early Church Fathers on some points. Since he could have obtained that part of his theology from them, we will have to consider the possibility that the essentials of Covenant Theology have been around since the first century.

John Calvin, along with Huldreich Zwingli, established the Reformed Church in Switzerland. John Knox later made Calvin's Reformed Church theology the basis for Presbyterian Church doctrine as well. Through the Anglican Church it even influenced Methodist, Congregational, Puritan, and Baptist theology. Consequently, Calvin's views on the two points of disagreement I mentioned above were *handed down* by Evangelists like John Wesley, Jonathan Edwards, and Charles Finney, as well as by a whole host of Baptist, Presbyterian, and Reformed theologians who taught theology in various seminaries both in the United States and in Europe.

Until the turn of the twentieth century, Princeton Theological Seminary, among others, provided the essential safeguards necessary to preserve intact Calvin's theological system here in the United States.

---

[10] See "The Protestant Confession: The Church Lost *The Teaching*," *The Voice of Elijah*, January 1992, and "Protestants All Agree on This: Somebody Laid an Egg!" *The Voice of Elijah*, January 1994.

Since that time, however, other seminaries have had to take up the banner in order to prevent Covenant Theology from succumbing to liberalism. That is why schools as divergent as Westminster Seminary in Philadelphia and Trinity Evangelical Divinity School in Deerfield, Illinois, still teach a theology that is based on Calvin's overall understanding of the biblical message.

So much for the rather straightforward history of Covenant Theology. Let's take a look at what John Calvin taught concerning the two essential points of disagreement I mentioned above: (1) the method one should use in interpreting the Scriptures, and (2) the relationship of Israel to the Church.

Covenant Theology in Brief

John Calvin believed the Scriptures *mean* what they say. Consequently, he was convinced True Believers should read the Bible as they would read any other book. Some parts were to be understood as speaking in a figurative sense, and other parts were to be understood as speaking *literally*. Calvin obviously believed the Scriptures and common sense combined would identify which statements were *meant* to be taken as figurative and which were to be understood *literally*. However, John Calvin, like Martin Luther, followed the dictum "Literal wherever possible."

It should be noted that Calvin did not get his view of how the Scriptures should be interpreted from Augustine. It's just as well. Augustine's view was more or less the same as that of Origen the Idiot, the moron who introduced the Church to the ridiculous allegorical method of interpretation.[11] In connection with John Calvin's view of how the Scriptures are to be understood, however, one must keep in mind the fact that he was absolutely convinced unregenerate individuals could not understand the Scriptures at all.[12]

On the issue of the relationship of Israel to the Church, Calvin held to the traditional Christian view that the Church is *spiritual* Israel. That is, he believed the Church has **inherited** the same **promises** and the same relationship to God that Israel had in the Old Testament. According to Calvin's Covenant Theology, the Church is now the covenant People of God. It is, in effect, the continuation of Israel, the People of God who held *The Promise* of God in the Old Testament.

---

[11] See "The Origen of Folly," *The Voice of Elijah*, January 1993.

[12] See "The Natural Man is an Idiot (When It Comes to the Truth)," *The Voice of Elijah*, October 1993.

Calvin derived his belief that the Church is *spiritual* Israel not only
from the Roman Catholic doctrine that prevailed in his own day but
also from reading the writings of Augustine. Augustine, in turn, must
have gotten it from his predecessors since it is the only view of the relationship of Israel to the Church that is ever expressed in the literature
of the Early Church. Consequently, we can say with some confidence
that, until 170 years ago, nobody in the Church had ever held a doctrine that taught anything other than the view of Covenant Theology
and the Early Church Fathers that the Church is *spiritual* Israel. In that
regard at least, John Calvin and all the other Reformers agreed the
Roman Catholic Church had never lost the Truth.

Concerning the Millennium, the Tribulation, the Antichrist, and
the Rapture, however, Calvin is distinctly a man of his times. In spite of
the fact that the Early Church Fathers were clearly premillennialists,
Calvin's favorite Church Father, Augustine, was an amillennialist. He
was, as I told you above, responsible for the Roman Catholic Church
adopting the amillennial view. Therefore, since John Calvin picked up
Augustine's views, he naturally assumed Revelation 20 symbolically
describes the Church as the promised kingdom of God on Earth. On
the basis of that belief, Calvin came to the conclusion that the Pope was
the Antichrist. Hence, he contended the Church was already suffering
the effects of the Great Tribulation.

Not many conservative Evangelicals today continue to hold Calvin's decidedly noneschatological beliefs concerning the future of the
Church. That is because the majority of Evangelicals have long since
abandoned Calvin's erroneous views on eschatology, realizing the
need to *restore* additional Truth about which Calvin had little to say.
Consequently, Calvin's amillennial position excludes him from the
premillennialists' discussion regarding the Tribulation and the timing
of the Rapture. But it certainly doesn't exclude the Early Church
Fathers. They were clearly premillennialists, and they have quite a lot
to say on the subject of the Tribulation and the Antichrist.[13] So before
we investigate the origin and doctrines of Dispensational Theology,
let's go back and take a look at how well Calvin's Covenant Theology
lines up with *The Teaching* of the Early Church Fathers before Origen
put his goofy spin on the Truth around A.D. 200.[14]

---

[13] See *The AntiChrist* and *The Advent of Christ and AntiChrist.*
[14] See "The Origen of Folly," *The Voice of Elijah,* January 1993.

The Early Church Fathers

I have already shown you that Church leaders prior to the time of Clement of Alexandria and Origen the Idiot had no real interest in interpreting the Scriptures for themselves.[15] That was because the leaders of the Early Church understood they were supposed to be *handing down* the things Jesus Christ had taught the Apostles.

In spite of their view that the mission of the Church was to preserve intact and *hand down The Apostolic Teaching*, however, Early Church Fathers were convinced that once True Believers had been instructed in the Truth, they could read and understand the Scriptures just as one would read and understand any other book. In that, they held a position somewhat similar to that of Martin Luther and John Calvin. So we can say that, with the exception of Luther and Calvin's misplaced confidence that God expected True Believers to read and interpret the Scriptures for themselves, the Reformers' view of how the Scriptures should be understood is fairly close to what the Early Church believed.

Since I have spent the better part of the past seven years[16] explaining the things I just mentioned, I won't bother presenting in this book the vast body of evidence that demonstrates their truthfulness. Anyone who is interested can read what I have already written. I have barely begun to demonstrate just how foreign the concept of interpreting Scripture was in the Early Church. By the time I have completed the task God has called me to, those who reject the logic of my position will have no excuse for not believing, other than the fact that they have arbitrarily chosen not to.

Now, let's take a look at what the Early Church Fathers taught concerning Calvin's contention that the Church is *spiritual* Israel. Those of you who have been reading my commentary on Justin Martyr's "Dialogue With Trypho" in *The Voice of Elijah Update* already know his view. John Calvin could have easily penned the comment Justin wrote less than seventy years after the last of the Apostles died:

> *For the true spiritual Israel, and descendants of Judah, Jacob, Isaac, and Abraham* (who in uncircumcision was approved of and blessed by God on account of his faith, and called the father of many nations), *are we who have been led to God through this crucified Christ.*[17]

---

[15] See "Did You *Mean* That Literally?" *The Voice of Elijah*, January 1993 and various articles in *The Voice of Elijah Update*.

[16] That is, from 1989 to 1996.

[17] Justin Martyr, "Dialogue With Trypho," xi, *The Ante-Nicene Fathers* [Roberts and Donaldson, 1867], Vol. 1, p. 200.

One has only to read with an open mind what Justin wrote about his conversation with the Jew Trypho to come to the decided opinion that the Church is the continuation of Israel as far as he is concerned. But Justin was not a lone voice crying in the wilderness of the second century. The Early Church Fathers are in unanimous agreement that the Church is in some sense Israel. They insist Christians are the recipients of *The Promise* God made to the Patriarchs. The author of the Epistle of Barnabas even gives a lengthy (although convoluted) explanation of how that came to be.[18] Irenæus, the most orthodox of all the Early Church Fathers and the one who defined the *meaning* of the term "heresy," tells us clearly how he understands the Church's relationship to Israel.

> *Now I have shown a short time ago that **the church is the seed of Abraham;** and for this reason, that we may know that He who in the New Testament "raises up from the stones children unto Abraham," is He who will gather, according to the Old Testament, those that shall be saved from all the nations.[19]*

Only a fool would dare deny that this pillar of the second-century Church firmly believed the Church was somehow the continuation of Israel, the Old Testament People of God. That is precisely the same point that Tertullian makes in his work titled "An Answer to the Jews."[20] Yet some might still choose to believe the Scriptures teach that the Church has no essential connection with Israel at all. Therefore, let me remind you the Apostle Paul plainly tells us the Jews have been "cut off from" the tree that *symbolically* represents Israel, and Christians have been "grafted in" to that same tree:

> *But if some of the branches were broken off, and you, being a wild olive, were grafted in among them and became partaker with them of the rich root of the olive tree, do not be arrogant toward the branches; but if you are arrogant, {remember that} it is not you who supports the root, but the root {supports} you. You will say then, "Branches were broken off so that I might be grafted in." Quite right, they were broken off for their unbelief, but you stand by your faith. Do not be conceited, but fear; for if God did not spare the natural*

---

[18] See "Given the Opportunity, the Fool Will Play the Fool," *The Voice of Elijah Update*, December 1993, or J. B. Lightfoot, *The Apostolic Fathers* [Grand Rapids: Baker Book House, n.d.], p. 137 ff.

[19] Irenæus, "Against Heresies," Book 5, xxxiv, *The Ante-Nicene Fathers* [Roberts and Donaldson, 1867], Vol. 1, pp. 563–4.

[20] See *The Ante-Nicene Fathers*, Vol. 3, pp. 151–73.

branches, neither will He spare you. Behold then the kindness and severity of God; to those who fell, severity, but to you, God's kindness, if you continue in His kindness; otherwise you also will be cut off. And they also, if they do not continue in their unbelief, will be grafted in; for God is able to graft them in again. For if you were cut off from what is by nature a wild olive tree, and were grafted contrary to nature into a cultivated olive tree, how much more shall these who are the natural {branches} be grafted into their own olive tree? (Romans 11:17–24)

I realize Satan has gone to great lengths to gain widespread acceptance for his own perverted interpretation of this passage. It's an integral part of his deception. That's why my very first publication was the book *Not All Israel Is Israel*. I suggest you read that book extremely carefully, then re-read it again and again until you fully understand the essential points I made there. It is the foundation on which I am going to build the message God called me to deliver to all those who seek to know the Truth in this generation. So if you can't understand the message of that book, or if you don't agree with it, I advise you to look elsewhere for whatever it is you seek. But should you choose to reject the central Truth I presented in *Not All Israel Is Israel*, I warn you: It is something Satan does not want you to believe.

Understand me clearly. Everything I teach is based on the fact that Jesus Christ is the Israel spoken of by the Prophets. As I explained in *Not All Israel Is Israel*, every Jew except Jesus Christ had been "cut off from" Israel by the time Israel—Jesus Christ—accepted the terms of the New Covenant when He was baptized by John the Baptist. There is, therefore, now no Israel other than Jesus Christ as far as God is concerned. That is why Paul says Christians, as members of the Body of Jesus Christ, have become joint heirs with Christ of **The Promise** that God made to the Patriarchs.[21]

The Early Church Fathers understood full well that unregenerate Jews are no longer a part of Israel. They knew the Jews had been "cut off from" Israel and Gentiles were being "grafted in." Yet idiots still try to refute what Paul wrote to True Believers at Rome:

For he is not a Jew who is one outwardly; neither is circumcision that which is outward in the flesh. But he is a Jew who is one inwardly; and circumcision is that which is of the heart, by the Spirit, not by the letter; and his praise is not from men, but from God. (Romans 2:28–29)

---

[21] Romans 8:17; Galatians 3:29; Ephesians 3:6; Titus 3:7; Hebrews 11:9.

If you want to state the case in the same way that John Calvin and Justin Martyr did, the Church is *spiritual* Israel. However, it would be best if you didn't do that. Use the *parabolic imagery* of the Scriptures that the Apostles and Prophets used and let it go at that: The Church, as the Body of Jesus Christ, is Israel. The designation *spiritual* Israel implies there is a *literal* Israel other than the Church (the Body of Jesus Christ) when, in fact, there isn't. It is true that, *parabolically* speaking, True Believers are members of the *spiritual* Body of Jesus Christ. So in that sense the Church is *spiritual* Israel. In every other sense, however, True Believers are—collectively—*literal* Israel because the *spiritual* Body of Jesus Christ is *literal* Israel.

So, you can see it was only the Reformers' fuzzy thinking in regard to the Jews and the Millennium that left the door open for Satan to entice some fool into crafting the goofy notion that the Jews are *literal* Israel. Satan picked his man 170 years ago, and he has been busy ever since making sure his lie is seen as the Gospel Truth by as many True Believers as possible. That's why I'm going to tell you what Satan's lie is and then explain how he intends to use it to shepherd billions of people into his deception when he appears as the Antichrist. That way, if you choose not to believe me, you will be responsible for your own destruction.

A Hint of Things to Come

Before I move on to describe how Satan has set in place the snare whereby he intends to deceive a vast multitude, let me briefly remind you what the Early Church Fathers Justin Martyr, Irenæus, and Hippolytus believed concerning the events that will occur here at the End. You can find their statements along with my own comments in *The AntiChrist, The Advent of Christ and AntiChrist,* and recent issues of *The Voice of Elijah Update.*[22] Since I have already published the writings of these men elsewhere, I will not quote what they said here. However, I will summarize their views to remind you of what they believed.

First of all, Justin Martyr clearly tells us the Second Coming of Jesus Christ will be heralded by an individual who, like John the Baptist, will be called "Elijah." Hippolytus agrees. However, Hippolytus provides a bit more detail about this person than Justin does. He says "Elijah" will appear shortly before the Antichrist comes on the scene.

---

[22] *The AntiChrist* is a condensed version of *The Advent of Christ and AntiChrist*, which was initially available only to those participating in the Monthly Contributor program sponsored by *The Voice of Elijah.*

He, along with another man called "Enoch," will warn the Church not to fall for the deception Satan plans to accomplish when he appears as the Antichrist. However, since Irenæus and Hippolytus both indicate most people will not heed the warning, we can assume the Early Church believed a majority of those in the Church would be taken in by Satan's deception.

As to the nature of the deception Satan has planned, both Irenæus and Hippolytus tell us it involves the claim the Antichrist makes concerning who he is. In agreement with what Jesus said in Matthew 24:23–25, they say Satan will come claiming to be the messiah of the Jews. After the Jews accept him as their messiah and make him king, he will rebuild the Temple in Jerusalem, sit on a throne in the Holy of Holies, and require worship from everyone as though he were Jesus Christ Himself.

Hippolytus tells us that those who have believed the warning of "Elijah" and "Enoch" will not fall for the deception of the Antichrist. Consequently, as both Irenæus and Hippolytus agree, those who know the Truth will be forced to endure horrible persecution during the Great Tribulation. Their suffering will continue for 3½ years, after which time they will be rescued by the Rapture shortly before the Second Coming of Jesus Christ.

From that brief survey you can see that, in contrast to the amillennial views of Augustine that John Calvin adopted, the Early Church Fathers were not only premillennialists, they were also posttribulationalists. An understanding of those facts will become extremely important to you if you ever intend to see through Satan's deception. Having said that, let me go on to show you the incredibly devious way that Satan has, over the past 170 years, paved the way for his appearance as the Antichrist by weaving his lie into the very fabric of Evangelical Protestant Church theology.

The Origin of Dispensational Theology

The man with whom the dispensational understanding of Scripture originated was an Irishman named John Nelson Darby. It is important to note that, in contrast to Covenant Theology, John Darby's dispensational ideas did not come together as a complete theological system. As formulated by Darby, dispensationalism was nothing more than a method for interpreting the prophetic literature of the Old Testament. His dumbness would not take the form of a complete systematic theology until more than a century later. That fact will have quite a bit of significance in our understanding of what Satan intends to accomplish by his ingenious deception, so you should take note of it.

John Darby was born on November 18, 1800, in London, England. That makes him a contemporary of both Søren Kierkegaard and Charles Finney.[23] Like Kierkegaard, Darby held an extremely low opinion of the Church and arrogantly assumed he could, by virture of his own intelligence, come up with a better understanding of the Scriptures.

Like both Kierkegaard and Finney, Darby provides us an account of his "conversion" experience. In it we find that, unlike Finney, he makes no mention of an honest repentance and acceptance of God's forgiveness. His is instead the unfocused account of how, after several years spent wrestling with the issue of salvation, he suddenly came to the realization one day that he was united with Christ in Heaven. That sounds a whole lot like Kierkegaard's hope-as-faith nonsense to me. But maybe I'm just biased against those who casually cast aside the tenets of historic Christianity in order to chase their tail around the Scriptures like a half-crazed dog.

Enough sarcasm. Let's go on to see if we can understand why so many in the nineteenth century Protestant Church found this weird little man so personally revolting, yet his interpretation of prophecy completely irresistible. As one writer who met him describes him, it sounds like he may have exuded a satanic aura:

> *In spite of the strong revulsion which I felt against some of the peculiarities of this remarkable man, I for the first time in my life found myself under the dominion of a superior. When I remember, how even those bowed down before him, who had been to him in the place of parents—accomplished and experienced minds,—I cease to wonder in the retrospect, that he riveted me in such bondage.*[24]

Please consider the merits of John Darby's position. He, like John Calvin and all the other Protestant Reformers, insisted some long-lost Truth needed to be *restored* before True Believers could be what God intended them to be. Moreover, he believed, like Luther, Calvin, Zwingli, Wesley, Williams, and countless other Protestant Reformers,

---

[23] See "Satan's Fools are Satan's Tools," *The Voice of Elijah*, April 1994 and "Charles Finney: My Conversion to Christ," *The Voice of Elijah*, January 1992.

[24] Francis W. Newman, *Phases of Faith, or, Passages from the History of My Creed* [London: John Chapman, 1850], p. 33, quoted by Clarence Bass, *Backgrounds to Dispensationalism* [Grand Rapids: Wm. B. Eerdmans, 1960], p. 54.

that he understood what Truth the Church had lost. In those respects at least, he was no less a Reformer than they.

Yet Darby lacked one thing that all these other Reformers quite obviously had. He lacked the confidence that he could find clues to what the Church had lost by searching the writings of an earlier generation of Christians. Every legitimate Protestant Reformer has had that confidence. That is why Calvin went back to base his beliefs on the things written by Augustine. That is the same reason Reformers after Calvin tried to *restore* things they believed had been lost before Augustine's time. But you must understand, Calvin and the other Reformers were seeking to *restore* the Truth they believed the Church had lost. They were not trying to come up with some entirely new Truth on their own.

Darby took a different approach—a more arrogant approach. He discarded the writings of the earlier eras altogether and went directly to the Scriptures instead, evidently thinking his own intelligence was so vastly superior to everyone else's that he did not need to seek confirmation from any earlier generation of Church leaders. His arrogance was so great, as a matter of fact, that he placed no value at all on the writings of the Early Church. Darby himself puts his view of the Early Church Fathers this way:

None are more untrustworthy on every fundamental subject than the mass of primitive Fathers.[25]

Pardon me while I offend Satan's own: That is the opinion of an abject idiot. Yet you will find it restated by dispensational writers today who tell us the Early Church Fathers had an "embryonic," "primitive," or "rudimentary" form of dispensationalism—thereby implying that Christianity took eighteen hundred years to evolve into their "we know better than they" idiocy. They convey the same arrogance every time they tell us dispensationalism "developed" over some span of time. That is a complete rejection of the beliefs that spawned the Protestant Reformation.

According to the traditional Protestant position, the Early Church had the Truth and lost it sometime after the Apostolic Age. Therefore, they saw the task of the Protestant theologian as an attempt to determine what Truth had been lost and to *restore* it. Dispensationalists ignorantly disregard this traditional Protestant belief and insist their goofy

---

[25] J. N. Darby, in W. Kelly (ed.), *The Collected Writings of J. N. Darby* [Sunbury, Pa.: Believers Bookshelf, 1971], Vol. 14, Ecc. No. 3, p. 68.

system is true in spite of the fact that they admit the Early Church Fathers never fully understood the doctrines of John Darby. Trust me on this one. Satan's dispensational understanding of prophecy is stupid. But Protestants who accept his idiocy over the Truth inherent in the what the Early Church Fathers wrote have no excuse. They should know better.

Perhaps the children of darkness who took offense at what I just said will find the assessment of the covenant theologian Clarence Bass more to their liking. He describes the arrogance of Darby and his dispensational followers a bit more tactfully. He has nonetheless succinctly captured the essence of the matter:

> **Darby's writings stand in sharp contrast with traditional views on eschatology.** *His spirit of independence from the scholarship of the past is best reflected by one of the opening statements in his prophetic writings.*[26]

That's putting it mildly. John Nelson Darby had as great a disdain for the Early Church Fathers as the fool Søren Kierkegaard had for Martin Luther and the other leaders of the Protestant Reformation. But you don't have to take my word for it. Bass goes on to quote what Darby himself said about the Early Church "Millenarians" like Irenæus and Hippolytus. In his words one can almost hear the complete disgust that Satan feels when confronted with the Truth these men of God in the Early Church clearly understood:

> *For my own part, if I were bound to receive all that has been said by the Millenarians, I would reject the whole system: but **their views and statements weigh with me not one feather.** But this does not hinder me from inquiring by the teaching of the same Spirit ... **what God has with infinite graciousness revealed to me concerning His dealing with the Church.** I confess I think the modern writers on prophecy justly chargeable with following their own thoughts hastily, and far too removed from the control of the Scripture ... They take some text or prophecy as a starting point, pursue these suggestions of their minds in connection with their general views previously adopted, but leave the results almost entirely untried by the direct testimony of the Word, affording us theories ... diverging into the absurdities.... There is not a single writer whose writings I have seen (unless it be the author of one short inquiry) who is not chargeable with this fault.*[27]

---

[26] Bass, p. 128.

[27] J. N. Darby, "Reflections Upon the Prophetic Inquiry, and the Views Advanced in It," pp. 6–7, quoted by Bass, p. 128.

If you were alert as you read what Darby wrote, you may have already noticed the reason why he felt no need to verify his doctrines by reading the writings of earlier generations of Church leaders. He refers to his views as "what God has with infinite graciousness revealed to me concerning His dealing with the Church." I've already given you my views on the subject of personal revelation.[28] People who seek personal revelation of any kind are getting into a risky business to begin with, but the machinations of the Liar make that activity somewhat like sitting astride a gently sloping razor blade without the benefit of a saddle. But enough about John Darby's revelation or obvious lack thereof. Let's see what the fool did with the life that God gave him.

Darby graduated from Trinity College Dublin in 1819 and practiced law for awhile before being ordained as a deacon in the Anglican Church in 1825. The next year he became an Anglican priest. By 1828, however, he had left the Church of England, seeking something far more satisfying than the dead orthodoxy he saw there. He apparently found what he sought by meeting with a group of disaffected members of the Church of England who had a few years earlier started the Brethren movement. This group was later to become known as the Plymouth Brethren.

I remind you again that Dispensational Theology did not originate as a complete systematic theology. It was at first nothing more than a method for interpreting the Old Testament prophecies concerning Israel. That is why Darby willingly adopted the views of the Plymouth Brethren concerning the proper mode of church worship and government. His only interest was in developing his own views concerning the future of the Church. That is an important point to remember if you want to understand how Satan plans to use Darby's twisted interpretation of the prophecies concerning Israel.

Not until 1947 did Lewis Sperry Chafer finally publish Darby's prophetic system as a systematic theology on the order of John Calvin's Covenant Theology. Therefore, the essence of Dispensational Theology was not, and still is not, directly concerned with the structure of church government or even, for that matter, the nature of God, man, or sin and salvation. Its central concern always has been, and always will be, eschatology. That is why dispensational views concerning the Antichrist and the Second Coming of Jesus Christ can be, and have been—by the unlearned and unsuspecting—attached to and/or assim-

---

[28] See *The Way, The Truth, The Life*, and "Mystics, Meatballs, and the Marvelous Works of God," *The Voice of Elijah*, April 1993.

ilated into a variety of other theological systems, including Calvin's own Covenant Theology. That is as Satan planned it.

Dispensationalism remained a prophetic system of thought for more than a century because Satan knew he would have to orchestrate a series of small steps in order to supplant traditional Christian beliefs with a new eschatological system. However, he also knew he could begin with a completely distorted method of interpreting prophecy because, as I have already indicated, Calvin's adoption of Augustine's amillennial views had left a gaping hole in Protestant doctrine. That is why John Darby and the Plymouth Brethren were not alone in their search for what many Protestants believed the Church had lost and still needed to *restore.*

Premillennialists in Darby's day were trying to plug the hole they had identified in the traditional Protestant view, but they kept coming up short because they did not understand how Jesus Christ had become Israel, the Firstborn Son of God and ***Heir of The Promise.*** Nonetheless, in a series of meetings in England from 1826 to 1830, premillennialists tried to pin down exactly what beliefs they held in common. In 1829, they published a report in which they agreed that some prophecies of Scripture predicted the restoration of the Jews to Palestine. Obviously, to have come to that conclusion, they must have identified the Jews as Israel. That may have been the catalyst that prompted Darby to publish his first work that same year. In it, he contended that every mention of Israel in the Prophets refers to the Jews.

A few years after Darby joined the Plymouth Brethren, Alexander Campbell and Barton Stone withdrew from the Baptists to form the Disciples of Christ (1830–32).[29] Other groups were also leaving the established churches, seeking something more than they had to offer. You can get a feel for the religious climate in that day from the doctrines taught by the marginally Christian and obviously heretical sects that originated about the same time that Darby came up with his goofiness.

Darby's era saw Joseph Smith's asinine claims contribute to Mormon beliefs (1830) and Judge Rutherford establish the foundations for what was later to become the Jehovah's Witnesses. In addition, one can trace the origin of Adventist beliefs back to William Miller, who began to publish his views on prophecy in 1831. The founders of all these groups had a decidedly prophetic interest in the message of the Scrip-

---

[29] See "Protestants All Agree on This: Somebody Laid an Egg!" *The Voice of Elijah*, January 1994.

tures. That is, they were all concerned with the Second Coming of Christ and the establishment of His millennial kingdom. So it is not surprising to find their contemporary, John Darby, busily crafting an entirely new understanding of things related to the appearance of the Antichrist and the millennial reign of Jesus Christ.

Dispensational Theology in Brief

Darby published his first article on the subject of prophecy in 1829. It was titled "Reflections Upon the Prophetic Inquiry, and the Views Advanced in It." There one can find clearly stated the dispensational doctrine that will forever separate Covenant Theology from Dispensational Theology. Darby flatly contradicted the one belief the Church had held from the beginning of its existence until that very day. That is the belief that the Church is *spiritual* Israel.

Darby insisted the Church is not related to Israel in any way. But he made it clear that by "Israel" he *meant* the Jews. *PAY ATTENTION NOW! THE BELIEF THAT THE JEWS ARE THE ISRAEL SPOKEN OF IN THE PROPHETS IS THE SINGLE MOST IMPORTANT LIE THAT SATAN WOULD HAVE YOU BELIEVE.* He desperately needs it to pull off his great deception. Considering how vital the belief is in Satan's plan, it is not surprising that Darby had it from the very beginning. It is, in fact, the sole foundation on which the dispensationalists' understanding of Scripture is built.

Seven years later, in 1836, Darby published "The Apostasy of the Successive Dispensations." In this work he put forward what Satan would have us believe are the basic underpinnings of dispensational thinking—that the Scriptures are an account of how God has attempted to redeem mankind in a series of "dispensations," only to have His every attempt end in failure. It is important that you realize this "dispensational" view of the Scriptural message is nothing more than a red herring Satan introduced to confuse people.

Dispensational Theology does not stand or fall on the basis of its dispensational framework. By no means! Dispensational theologians today will flatly tell you it is not important how many dispensations one can identify in the Scriptures. That is because Dispensational Theology has but one essential belief. That is the belief that the Jews are the "Israel" spoken of in the Prophets. As we have already seen, that concept is not at all in accord with the documented *Teaching* of the Church. And, as I have shown you in *Not All Israel Is Israel*, the Jews are certainly not the "Israel" spoken of by the Prophets. But, as we shall see later, it is not all that difficult to discern why Satan would have the Church believe that lie.

According to the prophetic system constructed by Darby, the Church is not mentioned even once in the Old Testament. Only Israel is. However, to Darby, Israel is always the Jews. That's how the dispensationalists got the distinction they make between the *Kingdom of Heaven* and the *Kingdom of God*. They believe the Church came into existence as sort of an afterthought after the Jews rejected Jesus Christ's offer to establish the earthly *Kingdom of God* among them as (they think) the Prophets had promised. When the Jews rejected His offer, Jesus Christ established the *Kingdom of Heaven* with the Gentiles instead of the *Kingdom of God* with the Jews. At His Second Coming, when the Jews accept Him as their Messiah, Jesus Christ will finally establish the earthly *Kingdom of God* with Israel—the Jews—just as (they think) the Prophets promised. He will then rebuild the Temple in Jerusalem, reinstitute the Temple sacrifices, and reign as king over the Jews. All the nations of the Earth will submit to Him.

If you are the least bit spiritually discerning, you can already see how Satan's lie will ensnare those who are unaware of the Truth that Irenæus and Hippolytus understood. Darby's description of Jesus Christ establishing His millennial kingdom over the Jews is exactly how these two Early Church Fathers describe Satan's appearance in the person of the Antichrist. If that eerie circumstance unsettles you a bit, you are one of the fortunate few. Most will respond, "So what?", never once realizing that Satan is standing right beside them, whispering in their ear, telling them exactly what he wants them to believe. No one ever heard that mesmerizing voice more clearly than John Nelson Darby. To read his writings is the surest way I know to gain insight into the Liar's plan.

In "The Hopes of the Church of God," which he published in 1840, Darby makes it clear that the Church and Israel (the Jews) have completely separate destinies. The Church is destined for a heavenly kingdom, Israel for an earthly one. But keep in mind the fact that he came to that conclusion on the basis of his *literal* method of interpreting the Prophets. In Darby's system, any time the Prophets mention Israel, they mean *literal* Israel, that is, the Jews. Hence, Darby and the other Brethren writers who promoted his system spoke in terms of the *literal* interpretation of the Scriptures when, in fact, they were actually arguing for what they believed was a *literal* understanding of the word "Israel" in the Prophets. They failed to understand that the collective *spiritual* Body of Jesus Christ—the Church—is just as much a *literal* body as the collective *spiritual* body of the Jews.

Satan has had a field day over the past 170 years provoking people in regard to Darby's ignorant *literal* interpretation of Scripture. After Darwin's theory of evolution was taken up by the liberal wing of the Protestant Church, Satan was able to turn the issue of the *literal* interpretation of the Scriptures into an absolute farce! The Truth is, most people realize they should read the Bible the same way they read every other book. Some parts are historical narrative, some poetic, and some personal missive. All three of those allow room for both *literal* and *figurative* expressions. So the method one uses to interpret the Scriptures is not even an issue. The sole obstacle to be overcome in understanding the message of the Scriptures is *understanding what the Scriptures are talking about.* Amazingly enough, once you understand that, you can read and understand them just as you would any other book. But I will explain all that another time.

Dispensational theologians today argue that their method of interpreting Scriptures is very little different than the *"literal* wherever possible" view of covenant theologians, except for the fact that they don't *spiritualize* the fulfillment of prophecy. And covenant theologians more or less agree with them, yet they still won't let dispensationalists off the hook of their *"literal* interpretation" heritage. Instead, they ridicule the ignorance of the rigid literalists with statements like ths:

> *We can best criticize the literalists by saying that none really exist! Their greatest inconsistency lies in the fact that all of them at one time or another interpret some passages of the Bible in a figurative or spiritual manner.*[30]

Actually, both sides are half right and half wrong in their dispute about the *literal* interpretation issue. The dispensationalists' contretemps over their leading proponents using basically the same method of interpreting Scripture as covenant theologians do is, and always has been, the result of their belief that the Jews are *literal* Israel. But try as they will, dispensationalists haven't yet figured out how to let go of the *literal* interpretation issue. That's because they still haven't realized that the only thing Darby wanted anyone to take *literally* in the Scriptures was his identification of the Jews as *literal* Israel.

Let me show you just how stupid Darby's *literal* interpretation argument actually is. Every dispensationalist, including Darby, has

---

[30] William E. Cox, *An Examination of Dispensationalism* [New Jersey: Presbyterian and Reformed Publishing Co., 1979], p. 26.

interpreted Ezekiel's vision of the valley of dry bones[31] *figuratively* and understood the resurrection of Israel as a *figurative* description of the *literal* restoration of the Jews to the land of Palestine. Yet that is the one passage that speaks most clearly in terms of the *parabolic imagery* related to the *literal* resurrection of Israel—that is, the *literal* resurrection of the Body of Jesus Christ!

So much for the dispensationalists and their goofy claim that they interpret the Scriptures *literally*. They interpret *literally* only when it suits their very specific and limited purpose, that is, when Satan wants them to understand "Israel" as "the Jews." The rest of the time they interpret the Scriptures just like everybody else. Some parts are *meant* to be understood *literally*, some parts *figuratively*. I'll admit Satan has used Darby's *literal* interpretation stupidity to herd a multitude of unsuspecting people into his snare. But he couldn't care less whether—as one sarcastic covenant theologian is fond of pointing out—anyone thinks they can *literally* pick grapes off Jesus just because He said He was a "vine."[32]

Two Views, One Point of Disagreement

Now you know the Truth about the two basic issues on which covenant and dispensational theologians say they disagree: (1) the method one should use in interpreting the Scriptures and (2) the relationship of Israel to the Church. As I just stated, the heart of the dispensationalists' interest in interpreting the Scriptures *literally* is their identification of the Jews as the *literal* Israel spoken of by the Prophets. So there is actually only one issue that separates Covenant Theology from Dispensational Theology. That is whether the Church or the Jews should be identified as Israel.

Covenant theologians adhere to the traditional Christian view that the Church is *spiritual* Israel. Dispensationalists ignorantly uphold Darby's claim that the Jews are *literal* Israel and there is no *spiritual* Israel. However, neither side has a completely accurate understanding of the Truth of the scriptural message. The Truth is, Jesus Christ is *literal* Israel, and the Church is *parabolically* His *spiritual* Body. Therefore, on that one issue at least, Covenant Theology has a somewhat better understanding of the Truth. That's not surprising. John Calvin had a greater regard for historic Christian beliefs than Darby the Dunce did. Yet in their silence concerning the future of the Church, Calvin and the

---

[31] Ezekiel 37.

[32] John 15:1.

other Reformers left the door wide open for Satan to use Darby's prophetic system to convince most of the Evangelical Church that the Jews are *literal* Israel and the Church should not be identified with Israel in any way.

Until Darby came up with his idiotic notion that the Jews are *literal* Israel, the Church had always identified itself as *spiritual* Israel, **Heir of The Promise** God made to Abraham, Isaac, and Jacob. But after Origen introduced his folly around A.D. 200, Satan was able to entice the Church into fuzzy thinking concerning the identity of *literal* Israel. Even John Calvin was sucked into that vortex by what Augustine had written. Consequently, he exhibited a decided ambivalence concerning the Jews and what, if any, role they continued to play in God's plan.

If you have read and believed the things I presented in *Not All Israel Is Israel*, you should already know that Darby's goofiness is nothing more than Satan's lie. According to the Scriptures, Jesus Christ is *literal* Israel, **Heir** to all **The Promises** of God. The Church is *spiritual* Israel only in the sense that it is *parabolically* the *spiritual* Body of Jesus Christ, the Body He took on at His resurrection. Therefore, contrary to what most folks believe, Jesus Christ is both *literal* Israel and *spiritual* Israel. And it is sheer blasphemy to say that unregenerate Jews are in any way still a part of Israel! But the Apostle Paul explains all those things in *parabolic imagery* that is simple enough for anyone to understand if they really want to. So let's go on to see how Satan has managed to convince most of the Evangelical Protestant Church that Darby's idiotic identification of the Jews as *literal* Israel is true.

The Rapture of the Saints

By the time Darby published "The Hopes of the Church of God" in 1840, he was clearly recognized as a leader among the Plymouth Brethren. Moreover, his beliefs concerning the future of the Church and Israel (the Jews) were well on their way to becoming the accepted view of Brethren everywhere. That gave him a solid base from which he could operate. So he traveled widely, visiting Brethren groups in Europe, Canada, and the United States. Everywhere he went he promoted his views on the future of Israel (the Jews) and the Church.

In 1845, not long after his new prophetic system gained ascendancy in the Brethren movement, Darby challenged B. W. Newton, the only other prominent leader among the Brethren, because Newton dared to disagree with one of his new doctrines. In that dispute we can see Satan desperately striving to make sure that essential part of his deception remained alive and well. It is fairly easy to see from what Irenæus and Hippolytus tell us that Satan certainly must not have been pleased when Newton adamantly rejected Darby's pretribulational Rapture of the saints! He needs folks in our time to believe what Newton refused to believe—that the Rapture could occur at "any moment."

Now, I must give credit where credit is due. Darby believed the Rapture of the Church would occur shortly before the appearance of the Antichrist. Yet dispensationalists stridently contend he did not get this doctrine from a group known as the Irvingites. It's interesting they should say that since Darby's dumb doctrine and that of the Irvingites are so obviously similar. The only other mention of a pretribulation Rapture of the Church before Edward Irving and his followers came up with it is a brief statement made by the premillennialist Joseph Mede in 1677. And his is not a full-blown doctrine. It's merely a conjecture he wrote in response to a question he received.

One can easily understand the dispensationalists' aversion to being linked to the Irvingites. Those folks were absolute lunatics. They were heavily into receiving revelation by means of prophetic utterances given during their meetings. That practice most likely accounts for Edward Irving spreading the good news in 1825 that the members of his Catholic Apostolic Church would soon restrain the power of the Antichrist for 3½ years before being martyred and ascending to Heaven. He also stated his followers would then return with Christ in the clouds of glory at the end of the 3½-year reign of the Antichrist. You can clearly see the doctrine of the pretribulational Rapture of the saints in what Irving preached. But you can also see why any good Evangelical Christian would not want to trace his or her beliefs back to that fanatic. Nonetheless, those who believe the pretribulational Rapture goofiness may well have to if Darby (as it appears) merely modified a doctrine he borrowed from Edward Irving.

Dispensationalists cannot deny that Darby had contacts with the Irvingites during prophetic conferences he attended in London during the 1830s. They nonetheless strongly deny he got the notion of an "any moment" Rapture of the Church from them. However, I can't help wondering how they can be so sure of that when Irving's stupidity must have been the talk of London in his day. But all that doesn't matter much one way or the other. Satan has seen to it that Christians in our time have been so thoroughly indoctrinated into the belief that Jesus Christ could come at "any moment" that most will not stop to consider it might not be true. Fewer still will bother to seek the Truth concerning the Antichrist in what Irenæus and Hippolytus recorded for our benefit. Those two leaders of the Early Church tell us the Church must endure the persecution of the Antichrist during the Tribulation. They say True Believers will be rescued only when Jesus Christ returns in the "clouds of glory" to destroy the Antichrist.

The stupidity of Darby in rejecting what the Early Church Fathers tell us is obvious when you consider the fact that Irenæus taught Hippolytus things he learned from men who studied under the Apostle John. He says those men told him John had taught them things he heard Jesus Christ Himself teach. So one must either believe what Irenæus and these other men said or else call them liars. I see no reason to do the latter. Therefore, I am left with the conclusion that what they say must be true.

Look at it logically: If ignorant men today can *hand down* the doctrines of a dunce like Darby for 170 years, why would anyone deny that the Early Church Fathers might have done exactly the same thing with *The Teaching* of Jesus Christ—especially when they tell us repeatedly that is what they were doing? I don't know about you, but frankly, I'd rather trust Irenæus and Hippolytus than some fool Irishman who thought he could figure out the message of the Scriptures for himself. Not that I have anything against Irishmen, you understand. My great-grandfather was one.

That's enough about Darby's goofy belief in the pretribulational Rapture of the saints. I'm sure those who have no "love of the Truth" the Early Church Fathers understood can come up with some extremely good reasons for continuing to believe as they do. So let's grant that what the dispensationalists claim is true, and Darby did come up with his "any moment" view of the Rapture on his own. If that's true, the Irvingite incident only illustrates how badly Satan wanted that doctrine put in play. One can easily understand why that is. It is an integral part of the deception he has planned for the Church here at the End. But enough of that, let's get back to tracing how the dumb doctrines of Darby the Dunce have become so widespread in the Church today.

The Spread of Dispensationalism

It should be noted that the nineteenth century was the era of the printed word in the same way that the twentieth century has been the era of radio and television. Darby was a master of that medium. He was not only a prolific writer himself, he constantly urged other Brethren leaders who agreed with him to write and publish as well. He encouraged those who didn't write to print and distribute what other Brethren had written. Consequently, during the last half of the nineteenth century, the leaders of the Brethren movement had an influence in the Evangelical Protestant Church that went far beyond what one would ordinarily expect of such a small group of men.

As a result of the recognition they gained among ministers who read their books and articles, Darby and his disciples—men like William Kelly, C. H. Macintosh, and William Trotter—gained access to the pulpit in various denominations. Once there, they preached the prophetic understanding of the Scriptures that had originated with John Darby. As Darby's prophetic views became more widely accepted, Darby himself came to have greater influence in other denominations. But few ministers were willing to openly admit their association with him or even to acknowledge their indebtedness to Darby and his disciples. That's understandable. The Plymouth Brethren carried a definite stigma because they did not have their own spiritual house in order. Again, that was the result of Darby's submission to Satan's leading.

After Newton disputed Darby's "any moment" view of the Rapture, the two had a series of nasty exchanges and then parted company. Shortly thereafter, Darby formed the "exclusive" Brethren. These folks tried to maintain the ostensible purity of their sect by refusing to fellowship with anyone who failed to maintain doctrinal unity. The net result of this practice, however, was the expulsion of anyone who disagreed with Darby on any issue. That served Satan's purposes quite nicely. It provided a way for him to protect and preserve his lie while Brethren leaders promoted it throughout the Church.

James H. Brookes was one of the ministers who was reticent to acknowledge his indebtedness to the Brethren. From 1864 to 1897, he served as pastor at two large Presbyterian churches in St. Louis, Missouri. Interestingly enough, over that period he illogically combined the basic premise behind John Calvin's Covenant Theology with the distinction that Darby drew between Israel and the Church. Moreover, the historical evidence indicates James H. Brookes remained completely dedicated to Satan's doctrine until the day he died. Satan must have found it a delicious irony that he could blind a Presbyterian to the point where he could not see the disparate nature of his own beliefs.

In December 1874, Brookes began publishing a monthly periodical titled *The Truth*. And in spite of his reluctance to publicly acknowledge his indebtedness to the Brethren, he regularly published articles in *The Truth* that were written by Brethren writers like H. H. Snell,

George F. Trench, John R. Caldwell, and William Lincoln. Moreover, Brookes repeatedly used his position as editor of *The Truth* to recommend things written by Brethren authors in England. Thus a strong case can be made that he most likely derived his dispensational views from reading what Darby and his followers had written. That is important only because some dispensationalists today would prefer to trace their roots only as far back as Brookes rather than all the way back to Darby. One can easily understand why. Not everyone holds Darby in the same high esteem that Brookes did:

> *A university graduate, and for years a clergyman, (he) was remarkable for his literary acquirements.... Those who sneer at him because he belonged to the Plymouth Brethren little dream that he surpassed them in scholarship us far as a giant surpasses a baby in strength.*[33]

It sounds to me like Brookes had also fallen under Darby's spell. That is not surprising inasmuch as he had plenty of opportunity. Darby preached from his pulpit on more than one occasion. So it doesn't matter much whether or not dispensationalists are willing to admit Brookes got his ideas directly from Darby. The evidence clearly indicates he had read Darby's books and accepted his dispensational ideas. As a matter of fact, Satan had reasons for Brookes hiding his indebtedness to Brethren writers. He wanted to, and did, use Brookes to ensure that Darby's deception was finally cut free from its identification as a Plymouth Brethren doctrine. The vehicle Brookes used as a cover for Satan's lie was the Niagara Bible Conference.

The Niagara Bible Conference

We have already seen how the Plymouth Brethren planted Darby's dumb doctrine in every Protestant denomination in the United States. Once that was accomplished, all that Satan needed was someone to make it his own and give it a little nurturing. James H. Brookes did all that and more. He helped to organize the Niagara Bible Conference and then served as its president from the time of its inception in 1878 until his death in 1897. Three years after Brookes died, in the fall of 1900, the organization closed its doors forever. So it is not too difficult to see that he was more than likely the driving force behind it while he was alive. By regularly bringing together those who believed,

---

[33] James H. Brookes, "Four Prophetic Periods," *The Truth*, XIX, April 1893, p. 200, cited by Daniel P. Fuller, "The Hermeneutics of Dispensationalism," doctoral dissertation [Chicago: NBTS, 1957], p. 80.

preached, and taught Satan's dispensational scheme, Brookes provided a convenient way for Satan to maintain his assault on all fronts.

Brookes and the men who helped him in the Niagara Bible Conference were nothing more than Satan's dupes. Evangelical critics of dispensational teaching in his day were correctly identifying dispensationalism as a Brethren doctrine and warning Christians that it was a dangerous innovation. Brookes and his fellow dispensationalists took offense at the mere suggestion that their beliefs might be in error. Consequently, they fought back with a vengeance. In the following quotation, Brookes not only reveals his complete ignorance concerning the premillennial/post-tribulation beliefs of the Early Church Fathers Irenæus and Hippolytus, he also provides a bit of insight into how difficult it would be for Satan to make headway as long as dispensational teaching continued to be identified with the Brethren:

> They claim that (the pretribulation rapture) is the Plymouth Brethren view, and, owing to the universal detestation with which this sect is held by all other sects, they use the argument with powerful effect on many shallow minds. But they forget that their own view is Plymouth Brethrenism. J. N. Darby and B. W. Newton had a quarrel more than fifty years ago, the latter a very able and scholarly man, becoming the founder of the doctrine that the church will pass through the tribulation.[34]

Brookes' argument against his opponents stems from his own ignorance. Newton was certainly not the origin of the Truth that Irenæus and Hippolytus taught. But you can still see from the tone of Brookes' statements that Satan needed a way to shift the focus of attention away from the Brethren and thereby take away one of the most potent arguments the critics of dispensationalism had: Nobody had ever heard of Darby's dispensational teaching until the Brethren began preaching it far and wide. Satan hated that argument, and he knew the only way to overcome it was to make dispensationalism a part of the Church at large. He had a plan whereby he intended to accomplish that, and a part of that plan involved driving True Believers out of the mainline denominations and into independent churches.

Now, Satan is a fool, but he is certainly not completely stupid. He knew that if dispensationalism remained restricted to only one identifiable group, the Church today would view it much the same way as it does Mormon teaching. But he also knew his new non-Christian

---

[34] James H. Brookes, "Who Shall Be Caught Up?" *The Truth*, XX, April 1894, p. 204, cited by Fuller, p. 82.

beliefs concerning Israel (the Jews) and the Church could sail success-
fully under the radar of all those on the lookout for non-Christian sects
like the Mormons and the Jehovah's Witnesses if they were broad-
casted throughout the Church under the guise of a prophetic system of
interpretation. To accomplish that, however, he needed a way for the
leaders of his new movement to meet regularly without being identified as a separate denomination. The Niagara Bible Conference provided that cover.

The meetings sponsored by the Niagara Bible Conference were
nothing more than a gathering of the leaders of a church within the
Church. And that is the way Brookes described them in *The Truth*.
However, he told people they were the gathering of the "wheat" from
among the "tares," implying that only those who attended his conference meetings were part of the true Church. That is just as Satan
planned it. He knew he had to appeal directly to those who actually
believed the Gospel. Brookes did an incredibly good job of it.

The proponents of dispensationalism continued gathering under
the guise of the interdenominational Niagara Bible Conference until
1900, when the organization disbanded. As I mentioned above, the
movement lost its focus almost immediately after Brookes died. Conference attendance diminished greatly and there was increasing controversy over Darby's doctrine of the "any moment" Rapture. But the
rapid demise of the Niagara Bible Conference is somewhat misleading.
The Truth is, Satan had already prepared someone else to assume the
role Brookes had played. Satan had groomed yet a third man for the
job of settling all controversy among dispensationalists by carefully
outlining the essential doctrines that he needs folks to believe here at
the End.

Arno C. Gaebelein

By the time James H. Brookes died in 1897, most of the original
founders of the Niagara Bible Conference had either died or left the
conference. The reason given by those who left was consistently the
same: They had changed their views on the "any moment" pretribulation Rapture of the saints. Men like Robert Cameron, Nathaniel West,
W. J. Eerdman, and others simply found they could not go on believing
a doctrine for which they found no evidence in Scripture. However,
their departure merely left room at the top for an energetic new leader
to assume command. And I have to admit Satan's new fool hit the
ground running.

Immediately after the Niagara Bible Conference disbanded, Arno C. Gaebelein announced he was planning to begin a new conference—the Seacliff Bible Conference—the following year. But in his publication *Our Hope*, he made it clear he would not allow anyone to speak at the conference if they did not believe the doctrine of the "any moment" pretribulation Rapture of the saints. Gaebelein had thrown down the gauntlet. Dispensational leaders who did not believe Darby's "any moment" Rapture tried to form a separate conference and failed. By contrast, Gaebelein's Seacliff Bible Conference was not only successful, it continued on for several years, enticing a multitude of unsuspecting Christian leaders into believing Darby's dumb doctrines.

It is not difficult to see why Gaebelein was absolutely adamant regarding the "any moment" Rapture of the saints. He was, for all intents and purposes, a member of the Plymouth Brethren. After emigrating from Germany in 1879, Gaebelein had become a Methodist minister. For several years he enjoyed a good measure of success evangelizing among the Jews in New York City. However, after three Brethren businessmen—a Mr. Ball, a Mr. Fitch, and a Mr. Pirie—introduced Gaebelein to what Darby and his followers taught concerning the future of the Jews, the Jews found his Christian message much more acceptable. (They still do, as a matter of fact. The Jews, after all, have been expecting the messiah that Darby preached for nearly two thousand years.) After becoming a dispensationalist, however, Gaebelein left the Methodist denomination and dedicated himself to spreading Brethren doctrine throughout the entire Church. He was the perfect man for Satan's plan. Although ostensibly a Methodist, he was actually a covert Brethren. You can get a feel for his mind-set from the way he talks about them:

Through these brethren beloved, I had become acquainted with the work of those able and godly men who were used in the great spiritual movement of Brethren in the early part of the nineteenth century, John Nelson Darby and others. I found in his writings, in the works of William Kelly, McIntosh, F. W. Grant, Bellett and others the soul food I needed. I esteem these men next to the Apostles in their sound and spiritual teaching.[35]

[35] A. C. Gaebelein, *Half a Century* [New York: Publication Office "Our Hope," 1930], pp. 84–85, cited by Fuller, p. 106.

Understand what I am saying: Dispensationalism today retains the same goofy "any moment" Rapture doctrine that Satan conveyed to Darby because Arno C. Gaebelein refused to have anything to do with dispensationalists who did not believe it. It is interesting to note that Gaebelein's rejection of those who disagreed with him is extremely reminiscent of how Darby reacted when Newman disputed that same belief. In both cases, Satan was absolutely insistent that the doctrine had to be maintained. It is not surprising that he fought so ferociously for it. He knows the lie concerning the pretribulation Rapture is one doctrine he absolutely must have if he is ever to pull off his deception. Yet there is much more to dispensationalism than its "any moment" pretribulational Rapture of the saints and the distinction it makes between Israel (the Jews) and the Church. To discover what Satan's essential doctrines are, however, one need only read the Scofield Reference Bible.

The Scofield Reference Bible

Have you ever seen a Scofield "Bible"? Some folks have, some haven't. For all I know, you may even be using one as a study Bible. You are fortunate if you have never used one, however. That has kept you from being exposed to the mesmerizing power of Satan. But then again, if you haven't seen this prime example of Satan's stupidity, you won't be able to fully appreciate why he would use such a vehicle for the distribution of his deceit. So, if you are one of the fortunate ones, the next time you are out and about, see if you can find a copy in a bookstore or library. Look it over carefully and see if you can figure out what purpose Satan has behind each comment. It should be an educational experience.

You see, the *Scofield Reference Bible* is a commentary—and a rather puny commentary at that. However, its brevity is intentional. Its primary purpose is to explain the dispensational interpretation of selected passages of Scripture in a way that can be easily understood by a layman. So why is it called a "Bible" instead of a "commentary"? Well, that's where the story gets extremely interesting. You see, Satan knew that, if he ever intended to succeed in "deceiving the whole world," he had to accomplish two things: (1) He had to get his deception into the minds of as many people as he possibly could, and (2) He had to make sure it had the greatest impact when it got there. The easiest way for him to do that in the early twentieth century was to bundle his deceit with the text of the Scriptures and call it a "Bible." So he enticed a mindless fool into doing exactly what the Scriptures warn us not to do:

I testify to everyone who hears the words of the prophecy of this book: if any-one adds to them, God shall add to him the plagues which are written in this book.
(Revelation 22:18)

Contrary to what idiots will argue, the Early Church understood that curse applies to the entirety of the Scriptures. Be that as it may, it certainly applies to the notes Mr. Scofield added to the Book of Revelation. Hence, I am certain he will have a few pointed questions to answer on Judgment Day. A multitude has been—and will be—led astray by his ingenious method of spoon-feeding poison to the unwary and unsuspecting. But enough about that. Let's take a look at how Satan accomplished what may well be his greatest deception to date.

Cyrus Ingerson Scofield was born in Michigan in 1843. However, he grew up in Tennessee and served in the Confederate Army as a decorated soldier during the Civil War. When the war ended, he moved to St. Louis where he studied law. After being admitted to the bar in Kansas, he served in the state legislature for several years. Then President Grant appointed him as U. S. Attorney to Kansas. That promotion was apparently not to his liking, however, as two years later he returned to St. Louis and began practicing law. That's where, in 1879, he made some sort of commitment to Jesus Christ and immediately fell under the influence of James H. Brookes.

Over the next three years, Brookes took Scofield under his wing and taught him everything he had learned about the interpretation of prophecy from Darby and the Plymouth Brethren. Thus it was, when Darby died in 1882, Satan had already groomed the man he intended to use to promote his deception after Brookes died. By the time Scofield took to the field, Brookes and his associates were working diligently to make sure Satan's deception spread like a cancer through the Evangelical wing of the Protestant Church. Yet C. I. Scofield and the *Scofield Reference Bible* would soon be responsible for the most rapid rate of growth that cancer has ever known.

In 1882, Scofield accepted the pastorate of a Congregational church in Dallas. He continued at that church until 1895, preaching sermons from the pulpit and teaching Bible classes in which he explained Darby's dispensational dumbness. Those who knew him tell us it was in Dallas that he came up with the idea of publishing his own notes alongside the biblical text and calling it a "Bible" instead of a "commentary." He surely must have known a commentary with no more academic heft than the one he planned would not have a gnat's chance of being taken seriously when compared to the tremendously detailed commentaries produced by the conservative Evangelical Christian scholars of that day. Therefore, Scofield could see he needed a gimmick. That's when Satan suggested the deceptive notion that he call his commentary a "Bible." Give Satan the credit he deserves. His deceitful tactic has been tremendously successful.

Scofield came up with the idea of writing a commentary and calling it a "Bible" long before he actually did it. That's most likely because he did not yet have the name recognition or the financial resources necessary to complete the project on the scale that Satan desired. Those two things would come later, after Scofield had—at the personal invitation of the Evangelist D. L. Moody—served as pastor of the Congregational church in East Northfield, Massachusetts for 12 years. Moody's relationship with Scofield is not surprising either. He had a long personal acquaintance with Darby and his Brethren followers, in spite of the fact that Darby openly expressed contempt for him. But that's another story.

By 1901, Scofield was recognized as an "elder statesman" on the Bible conference circuit. That is most likely how he came to meet Arno C. Gaebelein. When Gaebelein started his Seacliff Bible Conference in 1901 and rejected anyone who taught anything other than Darby's goofy "any moment" Rapture, Scofield hedged his bets by speaking at Gaebelein's conference as well as the conference held by the other group. From that we can tell Scofield's understanding of dispensational doctrine was essentially the same as Gaebelein's. That is probably why, when Scofield approached Gaebelein with his idea of publishing a dispensational "Bible," Gaebelein was all for it. As a matter of fact, Gaebelein just so happened to know a couple of businessmen who could fund the project.

Now who do you suppose would be willing to support Scofield financially while he wrote the commentary he disguised as a Bible? If you guessed the Brethren businessmen who introduced Gaebelein to Darby's writings, you are absolutely right. Mr. Ball and Mr. Pirie were more than delighted to see Darby's doctrine gain the recognition these men believed it so richly deserved. Consequently, the *Scofield Reference Bible* hit the stores in 1909, just as Satan had planned all along. Over the next thirty years, nearly two million copies were sold. As one researcher recently put it:

> *Friend and foe alike, credit* The Scofield Reference Bible *with being the single most influential force in the spread and popularization of dispensational and premillennial concepts up to the present day. It would be difficult indeed to estimate the scores of people who have been and still are being influenced by this early study Bible.*[36]

That just about says it all, in spite of the fact that it doesn't tell the whole story of Satan's deception. You see, not all of Scofield's new study "Bibles" were going into the hands of laypeople in the churches. By no means. Many of them became the single most important possession in the hands of a minister or someone who was preparing to enter the ministry. In the wisdom of God, that is exactly the way that Satan planned it. In fact, one of the basic reasons Satan's dispensational deception has become so closely identified with the Gospel is because Evangelists began preaching the Gospel right out of Satan's "Bible." Could anything have been more deceptive?

Evangelists and Dispensationalism

To fully understand how Satan has been able to pull off his grand scheme, one needs to understand the various ways he attacked the nineteenth-century Church. I cannot, in this short article, even begin to explain all that. I've already touched briefly on the controversy that erupted over Darwinism, but that was nothing more than a diversion. Darby played a role in that controversy by inciting a divisive side argument related to the *literal* interpretation of the Scriptures. But Satan's primary objective all along was to make sure dispensationalism became firmly fixed as "truth" in the minds of as many True Believers as possible. To do that, he knew he had to get it into that part of the Church that was experiencing revival.

Many of the Evangelists preaching around the turn of the century saw the mighty works of God as they preached the Gospel. As a result, they came to the mistaken assumption, as ignorant men always do, that God's divine imprimatur was stamped on their every belief and action. Nothing could be further from the Truth. After all, those who believed completely contrary doctrines saw exactly the same results when they proclaimed the Truth. Nonetheless, in the incredible wisdom of God, the Evangelists He called were responsible for combining

---

[36] Larry V. Crutchfield, *The Doctrine of Ages and Dispensations as Found in the Published Works of John Nelson Darby* (1800–1882), doctoral dissertation [Madison, N.J.: Drew University, 1985], p. 360.

WANNA HEAR A WHOPPER?

the Gospel with Satan's deception. In so doing, they made it possible for Satan to lead the conservative Evangelical wing of the Protestant Church down the path he had chosen for it to follow.

I have already mentioned Darby's association with the Evangelist D. L. Moody. That was only one of many links that Satan established between the advocates of dispensationalism and those promoting revivals. James H. Brookes actively cultivated ties with Evangelists from all segments of the Church through the Niagara Bible Conference. D. L. Moody did much the same thing. However, in later years he recruited and trained several young Evangelists to carry on his evangelistic work after him. Satan used these men to actively promote dispensationalism, along with a watered-down view of holiness, among the Evangelists who were preaching the Gospel in the Holiness Camp Meeting movement.[37] Therefore, as a result of calculated efforts on the part of James H. Brookes, C. I. Scofield, and D. L. Moody, many dedicated Holiness Evangelists like A. B. Simpson, as well as most of his tongues-speaking counterparts in the new Pentecostal movement, adopted Darby's dispensational views concerning the Second Coming.

By the turn of the century, most Evangelists preaching the Gospel had been taken in by dispensationalism. All that remained for Satan to do then was to use the "fundamentalism vs. liberalism" controversy to push the Evangelical Protestant Church from all sides until it amalgamated into one amorphous lump where doctrinal beliefs are not only no longer considered important, they are actually seen as an impediment to "Church unity" (whatever that is supposed to *mean*). Satan accomplished this during the second and third quarters of the twentieth century. Consequently, the dispensationalist view of the Second Coming has become just another belief on a smorgasbord of acceptable beliefs. Unfortunately, this particular belief is a deadly poison.

The Bible Institute Movement

How was it possible for Satan to reduce the Church, whose very foundation was once the Truth Jesus Christ taught the Apostles, to the rubble of conflicting notions it is today? Actually, it was not all that difficult. All he had to do was suggest a few innovative doctrines to specifically selected individuals who had no knowledge of, or regard for, Church history and traditional Christian doctrines. He could then use

---

[37] That is how Satan was able to inject the lie concerning "carnal Christians" and "spiritual Christians" into the Church.

the beliefs he crafted through these people to turn the Church in some new direction. That's all he did with Darby and his dippy doctrines.

To attain the measure of success he has enjoyed over the past two centuries, however, Satan knew he needed to foist his deception off on more than just a few people. He needed lots of folks who either did not know or did not care what the traditional beliefs of Christianity had been. Unfortunately, most of the people who believe his lie today fall into both categories. They don't know all that much about Church history because the people who teach them, like Darby, have a somewhat contemptuous attitude toward traditional Christianity. Consequently, the people being taught don't see why Church history is all that important. However, even that situation is the result of Satan's ingenious plan.

Over the past century, Satan has worked to create a mentality in most Christians wherein Church authority resides solely in the local congregation. Like dispensationalism, that is a novel concept. It can be traced back through the Plymouth Brethren to the Congregational denomination. Hence, it is no surprise that Satan used D. L. Moody and C. I. Scofield, both Congregational ministers, to push Darby's deception. The result of their efforts has been the rise of the independent local church. However, the independent church movement would not have been possible without another tool that Satan used— the Bible Institute. In this case, however, as in so many others, we find Satan and God using the same tool for completely different purposes.

By the end of the nineteenth century, Satan had already instilled in many Evangelical Protestants a deep-seated distrust of the doctrines taught in the theological seminaries of the mainline denominations. They had good reason to feel the way they did. Darwin's theory of evolution had long since contributed to the goofy belief that the Scriptures contain myth, saga, and legend. While Evangelicals watched in absolute amazement, their seminaries succumbed to the new liberal idiocy one by one.

Under such circumstances, it didn't take much for Satan to convince many, especially those involved in evangelistic outreach, that the best course of action was to take the Gospel message and cut loose from the traditional theological schools. But an additional argument he used to convince many is obvious: No denominational seminary in the United States at that time taught the premillennial doctrines of the Early Church Fathers, much less the goofy dispensational premillennialism of John Darby and the Plymouth Brethren. They were either teaching Augustine's amillennialism or the ridiculous postmillennialism that originated with Daniel Whitby (1638–1726).

By fostering multifaceted theological disputes, Satan was able to discredit the message coming out of the seminaries in the minds of many who still believed the Gospel. But his specific focus was those conservative theological schools that still had a respect for traditional Christianity. By lowering the esteem long accorded a theological education, Satan was able to bolster the image of dispensational schools which had little or no regard for traditional Christian beliefs.

Please understand: Without the safe haven provided by Bible Institutes, Bible Conferences, and the Holiness Camp Meeting movement, the vitality of the Gospel message might well have gotten lost in all the theological fuss that Satan kicked up. Therefore, all these new institutions played just as key a role in God's plan as they did in Satan's. The fact that God uses something, however, does not mean He places His unconditional seal of approval on it. As the saying goes, "Balaam was not the last person to hear God's message spoken by a jackass." God will most often use whatever moron is available (I should know). But enough sarcasm.

With new converts coming into the Church from revival meetings, the need for some kind of theological training for prospective leaders soon became obvious. That's when the idea arose that a one-year or two-year course of study at a Bible Institute could replace a traditional seven-year college and seminary education. Consequently, Evangelists and prominent ministers began to establish Bible Institutes outside the mainline denominations. This has, in large part, resulted in the "dumbing down" of Christians in regard to the history of the Church. That, in turn, has allowed Satan to introduce all sorts of ridiculous new doctrines without anyone asking whether they have ever existed before.

The Evangelist A. B. Simpson opened the first Bible Institute—Nyack Missionary College—in 1882. As the name implies, its purpose was to prepare individuals for missionary service around the world. From equally humble beginnings, many Bible Institutes have since gone on to become four-year liberal arts colleges. But it should be obvious that their original purpose was not to offer a well-rounded Christian education. It was to allow an opportunity for a few men to transfer their understanding of the Scriptures to several young people who were preparing for "the ministry."

One unique characteristic of the Bible Institute movement is the fact that it combined the Gospel message preached by conservative Evangelists with the dispensational doctrines of the Plymouth Brethren. While doctrinal teaching regarding God, man, Christ, sin and salvation, and the Church varied from institution to institution, the overwhelming majority of the Bible Institutes in existence by 1950 taught a dispensational understanding of the Second Coming. That is why the students at all these new Bible Institutes used a variety of theological textbooks, but after 1909 the majority most likely used only one study Bible—the *Scofield Reference Bible*. Is it any wonder then that, in the minds of a vast multitude of Evangelical Christians today, the Gospel is inextricably linked to a dispensational view of the Return of Jesus Christ?

Second Thoughts

As any True Believer should be able to see, the Church today is the product of nearly twenty centuries of spiritual warfare. The Evangelical wing of the Protestant Church—the only place where the Truth of the Gospel resides today—attests to that fact. It bears the marks of some of the most brutal spiritual battles the Church has ever lost. Yet, for the most part, the losses of the past two centuries have gone unnoticed because Satan has been able to convince True Believers that their loss was a win.

In this article, I have outlined a part of one of the most vicious running battles that Satan has ever waged against the people of God. I will eventually show you several of his other accomplishments as well. But those things are not all that important to us here. It is enough that you understand Satan was attacking the Church on several different fronts during the nineteenth century. His sole objective was to make sure that those folks who firmly believed the Gospel also believed several of his most deceptive lies. But he must have known his lies would never stick if he did not herd the Evangelical wing of the Protestant Church in a completely new direction. So that is what he did.

One of the primary ways Satan accomplished his objective was by driving a wedge between the intellect—a knowledge of the historical tenets of Christian theology—and the emotions—a personal commitment to Jesus Christ.[38] The net result of Satan's plan is that mainline theological seminaries today teach a dead orthodoxy that knows extremely little about a fervent belief in the *Living* Word of God while those who have experienced the life-transforming power of the new birth are exposed to some of the most fanciful and ridiculous notions that Satan could possibly devise.

---

[38] See "One Train. One Track. Two Rails." *The Voice of Elijah*, January 1992.

God has not called me to change the circumstances that exist in the Church today. Therefore, I am not arguing in favor of—or against—any one denomination, sect, or segment of the Church. My goals are actually quite simple. I am going to (1) explain how the Church got where it is, (2) explain the message of the Scriptures and show you it is the same message the Early Church Fathers understood, and (3) warn you to beware of Satan's deception. In short, I have been called to provide you access to the Truth you need to know in order to avoid an incredible catastrophe when Satan appears as the Antichrist. What you choose to do with the Truth I provide is your responsibility. However, if you have not already chosen to reject my message, you need to realize you are in a distinct minority.

As I warned you at the outset, if you have never considered the possibility that Satan might already have you believing his lies, you should begin now. Peter did not call Satan "the Adversary"[39] for no good reason. The primary target of Satan's unrelenting attention is, and always has been, anyone who seeks to know the Truth and follow God's will. That is, Satan is constantly standing against all who have experienced the new birth. Immediately after a person has heard the Truth concerning God's plan of salvation and has responded to it in the way that God requires, Satan attacks, using the arsenal of lies he has instilled in society over the years. His goal is always the same: To get the True Believer to deny some essential Truth he has already believed. If you were not aware of that, the chances are Satan has already deceived you in a variety of ways.

Satan has several extremely convincing lies at his disposal today. You are likely to hear one or more of them preached from the pulpit every Sunday. I hear them on the television all the time. For example, one of Satan's most incredible lies is the one that says doctrinal differences are not all that important, that it doesn't matter what you believe, it only matters that you have "professed Christ as your personal savior," or some such nonsense. Satan dearly loves that lie because the person who believes it cannot be saved. If it does not matter what you believe, salvation by faith is impossible. But enough of that, you get the idea: Satan works the Church like a politician would work a crowd of brand-new mothers, and don't you know that everybody's baby is just the cutest little thing?

Satan has various ways of enticing the unwary into believing a lie that will persuade them to give up some essential Truth. He doesn't

---

[39] 1 Peter 5:8.

have to work all that hard. The Truth of the Gospel is already accompanied by some of the goofiest beliefs you could ever imagine. So he most often just uses one of those. I have just shown you one of the lies he has at his disposal is Darby's dispensational teaching concerning events leading up to the Second Coming. While that goofiness has never been a serious threat to True Believers in the past, it is about to become one. So let me sketch a brief outline of dispensational beliefs concerning the Second Coming and then tell you what Satan intends to do with Darby's dumb doctrine.

A Glimpse Into Satan's Plan

If you have read and understood the first three chapters of the Book of Job, you already know that Satan does nothing without God's approval. That may be a hard one for you to swallow. It is true nonetheless. That *means* the things I am going to tell you about Satan's plan are things God must have approved three or four centuries ago. You may choose not to believe that. If that's your call, there's one other thing you should know: I'm just doing what God called me to do. That is, I'm letting a few folks in on Satan's plan so that they can avoid your fate.

There is only one way that you can avoid Satan's deception: (1) by being born again, (2) by seeing the Truth of the Scriptures for what it is, and (3) by remaining absolutely convinced that what you have seen in the Scriptures is true. Lacking any one of those basic requirements is a recipe for disaster. I realize not many today are naïve enough to believe that. So much for them ever becoming "like a child."

I mentioned before that the best way to gain insight into Satan's plan is to read what Darby wrote. I also told you the quickest way to do that same thing is to read the notes in the *Scofield Reference Bible*. Now I'm telling you the easiest way to confirm what Satan has in mind is to compare what Darby and Scofield wrote to determine what they hold in common. If you do that, you will come up with the following warped understanding of the sequence of the events that dispensationalists believe will lead up to the Second Coming:

1. THE RESTORATION OF THE JEWS TO THE LAND OF PALESTINE. I have already told you that, in the same year that Darby published his first work (1829), non-dispensational premillennialists declared their consensus of opinion that the prophecies of the Scriptures indicated the Jews would one day be restored to their homeland. Their identification of the Jews as *literal* Israel in these passages may well have been what set Darby off on his tangent. If it was, all Darby did was take their error to its logical conclusion. But regardless of how he came by his distorted belief, Darby and his disciple Scofield both believed the Jews would one day have a homeland. Keep in mind that was a long time before it actually happened. That "prediction" goes a long way toward convincing the unwary that dispensational teaching is true.

Dispensationalists today make much of what they see as a dispensational "fulfillment of prophecy" wherein a United Nations mandate made the modern nation of Israel a homeland for the Jews. It is doubtful that many of them are aware that was the expectation of nondispensational premillennialists before Darby ever came up with his goofy dispensationalism. It doesn't matter. Both the nineteenth-century premillennialists and the dispensationalists are wrong on this one. The Scriptures contain numerous recorded events that are merely a misleading "*parabolic* fulfillment" of the actual event predicted.[40] That is the case here as well.

The return of the Jews to Palestine is not the event predicted in those passages of Scripture from which the premillennialists and dispensationalists got their belief. The Second Coming of Jesus Christ is. Yet, firmly convinced of Satan's lie, dispensationalists will undoubtedly reject that notion outright, never realizing the restoration of Israel speaks *parabolically* concerning Jesus Christ returning to the land that is rightfully His as *the Heir of the Promise*.

2. THE APOSTASY OF THE CHURCH. Both Darby and Scofield tell us an Apostasy of professing Christians will signal the beginning of the End. The only difference between the two men is Darby believed the Church in his day was already in a state of apostasy, but Scofield believed the apostasy was yet to come. Both have a somewhat nebulous notion as to what could cause a mass "falling away" of Believers.

3. THE RAPTURE/RESURRECTION OF SAINTS. Both men teach that all Believers who have not fallen away during the Apostasy of the Church will be taken up in the Rapture. The dead saints from all ages past will be resurrected to join them in flight. Darby and Scofield both insist the Rapture will occur before the Antichrist appears. This is exactly the way Satan wants it understood. Darby makes a clear distinction between the Rapture and the Second Coming of Christ, saying Christ

---

[40] See "Is Iraq Mystery Babylon?" *The Voice of Elijah*, January 1991.

will come for the saints at the time of the Rapture and He will return *with* the saints at the Second Coming.

4. *THE ANTICHRIST AND THE TRIBULATION.* This is where the goofiness these men believed begins to get rather attractive to the simpleminded. Both agree there will be a Tribulation, and both claim it will be a 3½-year period in which the Jews living in "the land of Judah" will become the object of persecution by the Antichrist. However, Scofield calls this "the Great Tribulation" and includes an additional 3½-year period immediately before it in which the Antichrist will allow the Jews in Palestine to live in relative peace. Hence, Darby would place the Rapture 3½ years later than Scofield. That is a minor variance, however, since both believe the Rapture comes before the Tribulation. And both are emphatic on the point that the Jews, not the Church, are the object of the Antichrist's persecution.

Darby and Scofield also tell us the Antichrist will reign over a realm they identify as the "revived Roman Empire." Interestingly enough, they came to that conclusion on the basis of the *parabolic imagery* they found in the Books of Daniel and Revelation. The Early Church Fathers Hippolytus, Irenæus, and Tertullian confirm the dispensationalists' general understanding of that imagery. Some dispensationalists more logically expect the Antichrist to rule over a ten-nation "Mediterranean" confederacy. However, other dispensationalists today expect the Antichrist to be a leader of the European Common Market—after it finally gets its act together. Satan has apparently convinced them the "revived Roman Empire" is a modified restoration of the Holy Roman Empire instead of a restoration of the Roman Empire as it was when Christ died. Therefore, these dispensationalists expect the Antichrist to appear in the wrong place.[41] Their mistake will be costly.

5. *THE PREPARATION OF A JEWISH REMNANT TO ACCEPT JESUS CHRIST AS MESSIAH.* Both Darby and Scofield agree that a Remnant of Israel (the Jews) will come out of the Tribulation expecting Jesus Christ to appear as the Messiah of the Jews. Scofield plainly tells us this "remnant" will be comprised of Jews who have accepted Jesus Christ as the Messiah of the Jews during the Tribulation. This is, according to dispensationalists, the fulfillment of Romans 11:25–26.

---

[41] See "That's Why He's Called AntiChrist!" *The Voice of Elijah*, April 1992.

6. THE RETURN OF JESUS CHRIST AND THE BATTLE OF ARMAGEDDON.
Both men agree that, at the conclusion of the 3½-year period of Tribulation, Jesus Christ will return. He will set foot on the Mount of Olives and identify Himself not as Jesus Christ but as the Messiah of the Jews. He will then destroy the forces of the Antichrist in the great battle of Armegeddon as described in Revelation 19:17–21.

7. THE ESTABLISHMENT OF THE MILLENNIAL KINGDOM. The final series of events is something on which both Darby and Scofield are in definite agreement, in spite of the fact that dispensationalists today have distorted Satan's original message somewhat. After the battle of Armageddon, Jesus Christ will rebuild the Temple in Jerusalem. He will then re-establish the temple cult in which the Jews will offer "memorial sacrifices" in memory of His death on the cross. After rebuilding the Temple, He will purge His kingdom of all infidels and reign in Jerusalem over Israel (the Jews) for one thousand years.[42]

Satan's Planned Deception

I began this article by quoting five verses that tell us Satan intends to "deceive the whole world" when he comes in the person of the Antichrist. One of those was Jesus' warning that Satan's deception will involve someone pretending to be the Messiah. That agrees with what Paul wrote in 1 Thessalonians 2:1 ff. Later, I reminded you that the Early Church Fathers Irenæus and Hippolytus said the same thing about Satan's planned deception. Both men insist the Jews will accept the Antichrist as their messiah. However, the Early Church Father Hippolytus describes the Tribulation and the reign of the Antichrist in quite a bit more detail than Irenæus. And his explanation sheds an incredibly brilliant light on Satan's plan.

Hippolytus tells us the Antichrist will pretend to be Jesus Christ and the Jews will accept him as their messiah. Then he, not Jesus Christ as Darby and Scofield expected, will rebuild the Temple in Jerusalem and sit in the Holy of Holies, reigning as king over the Jews. Therefore, to understand what Satan's plans are when he appears as the Antichrist, all you need do is read Darby and Scofield, mentally substituting the Antichrist for Jesus Christ.

In case you are a bit dimwitted, let me put it to you plainly: *THE MESSIAH THE DISPENSATIONALISTS TELL US WILL DELIVER THE JEWS IS THE*

---

[42] Revelation 20:1–3.

ANTICHRIST![43] Just wait. You'll see. Satan fully intends to become the messiah the Jews have been expecting for nearly two thousand years. Unfortunately for all the Pretenders in the Church, he is exactly the same messiah the dispensationalists have been preaching for the past 170 years. And, to get us from here to there, I have no doubt God is going to give the dispensationalists precisely what they have been expecting.

I dare say some ten-nation confederacy will soon become the "revived Roman Empire" the dispensationalists expect. It doesn't matter much whether this is the European Common Market or a more nebulous "Mediterranean" confederacy. An individual they can identify as the Antichrist will head that confederation and support a military occupation of Palestinian territories to ensure the nation of Israel complies with an agreement it made. During this time of Jewish "tribulation," a "remnant" of Jews will likely respond to the "gospel" message of dispensationalism. Then, when the Jews in the land of Israel are facing some extremely tense situation, Satan's carefully planned deception will absolutely confound the world. I trust you will have prepared for it by then…

A Final Warning

If you haven't yet read what the Early Church Fathers Irenæus and Hippolytus wrote concerning the Antichrist, that is the place to begin.[44] They knew what they were *talking about* because the things they understood had been *handed down* to them by men who got it directly from the Apostle John. John had good reason to understand things related to the Antichrist. He wrote the definitive work on the subject—the Book of Revelation. So he was the one man best qualified to explain the *meaning* of all the symbols you find there. Nonetheless, most people today will readily disregard what his disciples Irenæus and Hippolytus wrote in order to believe John Darby's idiocy. That is a shame. Unfortunately, it is also a tacit admission that they have no "love of the Truth." Since I can obviously do nothing to change that, their fate will be exactly what the Apostle Paul described:

---

[43] To make it easier for you to understand the Truth, the chart on pages 54–55 compares the dispensational view of the Second Coming with that of the Early Church Fathers.

[44] I have published everything Irenæus and Hippolytus wrote about the Antichrist (along with my comments in the footnotes) in a book titled *The Advent of Christ and Anti-Christ*, which is available only through *The Voice of Elijah*.

*And then that lawless one will be revealed whom the Lord will slay with the breath of His mouth and bring to an end by the appearance of His coming; {that is,} the one whose coming is in accord with the activity of Satan, with all power and signs and false wonders, and with all the deception of wickedness for those who perish, **because they did not receive the love of the truth so as to be saved. And for this reason God will send upon them a deluding influence so that they might believe what is false, in order that they all may be judged who did not believe the truth, but took pleasure in wickedness.***
(2 Thessalonians 2:8–12)

Final Comments

Since I began writing this article, I've had some difficulty deciding what to include and what not to include. For example, I thought about explaining how Satan is currently working in the Church and the media to shape the mentality of this generation in preparation for his appearance as the Antichrist. However, that is not pertinent to my purpose here. I have barely taken you past the first decade of the twentieth century. How can I expect you to understand how Satan is working right now if you are not aware of how we got to "right now"? Therefore, I won't explain how Hal Lindsey's phenomenal best-seller, *The Late Great Planet Earth* (100,000,000 copies sold!) and all those "Rapture" movies being shown in the churches fit into Satan's plan. Nor will I tell you why Satan fought so hard to retain the doctrine of the "any moment" Rapture.

I also thought about giving you a more detailed explanation of the events that will lead up to Satan's appearance. But that would serve little purpose if you are not fully convinced by what I've told you here. So I'll explain all that another time as well, after you've had opportunity to form an opinion as to whether or not *The House* message is true.

However, there is one thing I feel I should tell you: When I say things like "Darby's dumb doctrines" and "Satan's stupid system," I do it only because I like alliteration. (I'm kidding!) Actually, I am mocking the stupidity of ignorant men because God has called me to do that. I realize those who are ignorant will never be able to accept my claim that God called me to ridicule people, but how could they? They can't see that Jesus Christ, the Prophets, and the Apostles did the same thing. So what good would it do for me to point it out to them? Please understand me: God has not called me to teach those who are concerned about appearances. He has called me to make the Truth available to those who are seeking Truth. Mockery will turn back the majority of those who read what I write because proud people will have a difficult time taking me seriously. Therefore, my ridicule is testimony to the intensity of the burning wrath of God.

Those who love the Truth more than decorum have no difficulty at all getting past my ridicule of those who casually believe whatever sounds good without any consideration at all of whether or not it is actually true. Everybody who wants to cling to Satan's lies will take immediate offense at my disparagement of those who tenaciously cling to ignorant beliefs, as though I had attacked them personally. They fail to understand I merely pointed out the stupidity of their belief system. I didn't tell them they had to believe it. They were dumb enough to do that all by themselves. If you have heard the Truth in what I say, you already know my ridiculing of stupidity is no impediment to your understanding the Truth of what I say. That is as God has planned it. The Prophet Daniel described the "winnowing" process this way:

> As for me, I heard but could not understand; so I said, "My lord, what {will be} the outcome of these {events}?" "Go {your way}, Daniel, for {these} words are concealed and sealed up until the end time. **Many will be purged, purified and refined; but the wicked will act wickedly, and none of the wicked will understand, but those who have insight will understand.** And from the time that the regular sacrifice is abolished, and the abomination of desolation is set up, {there will be} 1,290 days. How blessed is he who keeps waiting and attains to the 1,335 days! But as for you, go {your way} to the end; then you will enter into rest and rise {again} for your allotted portion at the end of the age."
> (Daniel 12:8–13)

In His wrath, God has called me to provide "insight" to "the Many" openly so that anyone who wants to know the Truth can finally understand what He has done in history. However, since most people today have already been completely taken in by Satan's stupid god of unconditional grace, you probably don't believe that either. Therefore, let me tell you a few other things you won't believe.

I am currently putting together all the information the Elect of God will need in order to avoid being taken in by Satan's delusion. Please understand me: I am merely providing information. That is all that God has called me to do. I am not gathering people together in some new "sect," "denomination," "church," or "cult." Therefore, the agents of Satan will readily identify themselves by warning everyone not to listen to what I teach because it is "cultic." You really should heed what they say. The things I teach are incredibly subversive. They have the power to completely control you—if you believe them.

As I have told you before, God has hidden seven complete messages in the Hebrew Scriptures. I have been called to explain all seven of those messages in a form that is understandable to a layperson. I must then make that explanation available to anyone who wants to read it. As is obvious, it will not only take me several years to complete my calling, it will also take substantial financial backing. That is the purpose of The Next Step program. The Next Step participants are assisting me by providing extraordinary contributions to *The Voice of Elijah*. I want to thank them publicly for their commitment. The things I am teaching them in that program are the driving force behind my own growth in an understanding of the Truth.

Over the next several years, I am also going to publish the writings of the Early Church Fathers along with my own comments. I am doing that in segments and publishing those segments in *The Voice of Elijah Update*. The Monthly Contributors to *The Voice of Elijah* are providing financial support for that project, which will most likely continue for at least the next decade. My purpose in commenting on the Early Church Fathers is to demonstrate that they understood exactly the same things I am going to show you God has hidden in the Hebrew Scriptures.

I am also going to provide a bit more insight into how Satan has achieved his goals in the Church over the past three or four centuries. I will do that in the pages of this newsletter. So if you found this article entertaining and want to enjoy a few more laughs at the expense of a religious fanatic, feel free to tag along. It should be an interesting ride, and I'm sure you will, somewhere along the way, discover whatever version of the "truth" you are seeking.

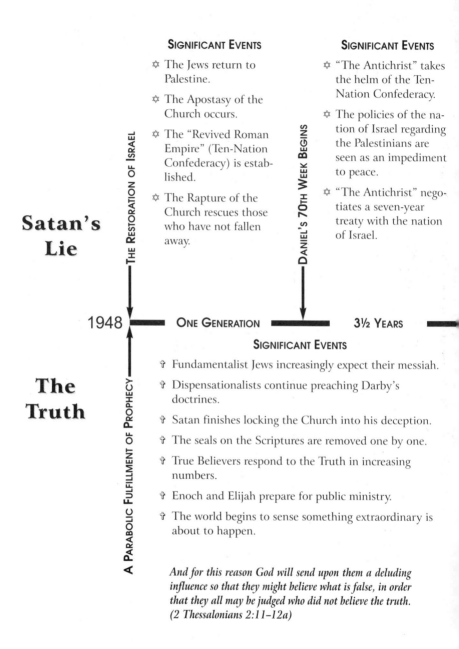

SIGNIFICANT EVENTS

✡ The Jews return to Palestine.

✡ The Apostasy of the Church occurs.

✡ The "Revived Roman Empire" (Ten-Nation Confederacy) is established.

✡ The Rapture of the Church rescues those who have not fallen away.

SIGNIFICANT EVENTS

✡ "The Antichrist" takes the helm of the Ten-Nation Confederacy.

✡ The policies of the nation of Israel regarding the Palestinians are seen as an impediment to peace.

✡ "The Antichrist" negotiates a seven-year treaty with the nation of Israel.

Satan's Lie

THE RESTORATION OF ISRAEL

DANIEL'S 70TH WEEK BEGINS

1948 ■ **ONE GENERATION** ■ **3½ YEARS** ■

The Truth

A PARABOLIC FULFILLMENT OF PROPHECY

SIGNIFICANT EVENTS

✞ Fundamentalist Jews increasingly expect their messiah.

✞ Dispensationalists continue preaching Darby's doctrines.

✞ Satan finishes locking the Church into his deception.

✞ The seals on the Scriptures are removed one by one.

✞ True Believers respond to the Truth in increasing numbers.

✞ Enoch and Elijah prepare for public ministry.

✞ The world begins to sense something extraordinary is about to happen.

And for this reason God will send upon them a deluding influence so that they might believe what is false, in order that they all may be judged who did not believe the truth. (2 Thessalonians 2:11–12a)

SIGNIFICANT EVENTS (left column)

✿ World opinion turns against the nation of Israel.

✿ A united world force comes against the nation of Israel to force compliance on the Palestinian issue.

✿ A new dispensational "gospel" is preached to the Jews.

✿ A "remnant" of the Jews prepares for the Return of Jesus Christ.

Left margin label: **THE GREAT TRIBULATION BEGINS**

SIGNIFICANT EVENTS (right column)

✿ "Jesus Christ" descends on the Mount of Olives.

✿ The Jews accept "Jesus Christ" as their Messiah.

✿ Christians are told they have missed the Rapture.

✿ The Temple is rebuilt.

✿ The sacrificial rituals are re-established.

✿ "Jesus Christ" ascends to the throne in the Holy of Holies.

✿ The millennial reign of "Jesus Christ" begins.

✿ The entire world is required to worship "Jesus Christ."

✿ Those who refuse to worship are hunted down and executed.

Center margin label: **"JESUS CHRIST" RETURNS**

3½ YEARS   **3½ YEARS**

SIGNIFICANT EVENTS (lower left column)

✠ Enoch and Elijah openly explain the message of the Scriptures.

✠ Everyone is warned concerning Satan's planned deception.

✠ Most "Christians" angrily reject the Truth.

✠ The Elect prepare to flee in order to avoid capture and execution by the forces of the Antichrist.

Left margin label: **DANIEL'S 70TH WEEK BEGINS**

SIGNIFICANT EVENTS (lower right column)

✠ Satan descends on the Mount of Olives.

✠ The Jews accept him as their messiah.

✠ The Apostasy of the Church begins as most True Believers believe Satan's deception.

✠ The Temple is rebuilt.

✠ The sacrificial rituals are re-established.

✠ The Antichrist sits on a throne in the Holy of Holies as the "abomination of desolation."

✠ The reign of the Antichrist begins.

✠ The whole world is required to accept the Mark of the Beast and worship the Antichrist.

✠ Only those who know the Truth refuse to worship.

✠ Those who refuse are hunted down and executed.

✠ A Remnant is rescued by the Rapture immediately before the Second Coming.

Center margin label: **THE GREAT TRIBULATION BEGINS**

Right margin label: **THE RESTORATION OF ISRAEL (JESUS CHRIST RETURNS)**